DATE			

MERTON

By Those Who
Knew Him Best

MERTON

By Those Who Knew Him Best

Edited by Paul Wilkes

1817

Harper & Row, Publishers, San Francisco

Cambridge, Hagerstown, New York, Philadelphia,
London, Mexico City, São Paulo, Singapore, Sydney

Published in conjunction with the Thomas Merton Center for Religious Studies at Columbia University and the Merton Project.

Grateful acknowledgement is made for permission to use excerpts from the following publications by Thomas Merton: *The Sign of Jonas,* copyright 1953 by The Abbey of Our Lady of Gethsemani; renewed 1981 by The Trustees of the Merton Legacy Trust. Reprinted by permission of Harcourt Brace Jovanovich, Inc. *The Seven Storey Mountain,* copyright 1948 by Harcourt Brace Jovanovich, Inc.; renewed 1976 by The Trustees of the Merton Legacy Trust. Reprinted by permission of the publisher. *The Asian Journal of Thomas Merton,* copyright © 1968, 1970, 1973 by The Trustees of the Merton Legacy Trust. Reprinted by permission of New Directions Publishing Corporation. *New Seeds of Contemplation,* copyright © 1961 by the Abbey of Gethsemani, Inc. Reprinted by permission of New Directions Publishing Corporation. *Conjectures of Guilty Bystander,* copyright © 1966 by Doubleday & Company, Inc. Reprinted by permission of Doubleday & Company, Inc. *The Nonviolent Alternative,* copyright © 1980 by Farrar, Straus & Giroux. *The Silent Life,* copyright © 1975 by Farrar, Straus & Giroux. Both reprinted by permission of Farrar, Straus & Giroux. *Merton: A Pictorial Biography,* copyright © 1980 by The Paulist Press. Reprint by permission of The Paulist Press.

All photographs by Paul Wilkes, unless otherwise indicated.

FIRST EDITION

Designer: Jim Mennick

Library of Congress Cataloging in Publication Data

Main entry under title:
MERTON, BY THOSE WHO KNEW HIM BEST.

Bibliography: p.
1. Merton, Thomas, 1915–1968—Addresses, essays, lectures. 2. Monks—United States—Biography—addresses, essays, lectures. 3. Trappists—United States—Biography—Addresses, essays, lectures. I. Wilkes, Paul, 1938–
BX4705.M542M39 1984   271'.125'024 [B]   84-47824
ISBN 0-06-069416-5

85 86 87 88 10 9 8 7 6 5 4 3 2

Contents

Introduction

For a man who spent half his life in a cloistered Trappist monastery, Thomas Merton had an amazing number and variety of friends. To term them *acquaintances* or anything else would dilute the passion and fervor Thomas Merton invested in them—and they in him. Throughout his life, Merton was never a moderate man—disciplined, yes, but never moderate. And as actively as he pursued the transcendent God, he cultivated and cherished a wide range of earthly men and women.

Merton's friends filled many roles in his life. To some he could talk or write about Cistercian spirituality; to others, the horrors of nuclear war; with some he engaged in the most erudite conversations about Mahayana Buddhism or the wisdom of the ancient Desert Fathers. And to still others he quite frankly complained of the rigors, pressures, and irritations of life within his monastic community. Merton had an enormous range of interests, and the diversity of his friends fed and kept alive his fertile intellect.

It is no small paradox that, while Thomas Merton yearned for solitude throughout his life, and in fact was living as a hermit in his last years, he had an equally great need for human interchange. His secular friends were his eyes and ears to the world from which he had excluded himself. They sent him books and clippings and letters in such volume that the censors at the Abbey of Our Lady of Gethsemani eventually just gave up trying to screen his mail. His friends brought him picnic lunches and beer, spiriting a not unwilling abductee off for hillside banquets and rides along the Kentucky back roads. Merton's private journals bemoan the incursions of so many people, the press of his mail, his inability to say no to requests for an essay on this subject or that problem, but clearly he relished this apparently conflicting aspect of his contemplative life. And he was not above bending Gethsemani rules so that he might see those people he wanted to and avoid those—usually the too ardent or adoring—he did not.

While his conversations with his friends and letters to them were sometimes quite specific, intellectually rigorous, and issue oriented, everyone who knew him well says that Thomas Merton —or Father Louis, as he was known within the Gethsemani community—was an exceptionally easy person to be with. Over and over again in my interviews, Merton's closest and even his casual friends have laughed and recalled how, in his presence, each of them felt assured of a special place in his life. Merton made each one feel that his or her friendship, visit, or letter was of the greatest importance. And they laughed at such recollections because they had often heard the same sense of acknowledged significance expressed by still another of his disparate friends.

What picture of Thomas Merton emerges as these many friends, from different religions, races, and walks of life, talk about him? Well, first if he was a holy man—as his mystical writings surely imply—he was anything but a plaster-cast saint. There was nothing sanctimonious or ethereal about him. He laughed a lot. Merton was a man without guile, not good at masking his feelings, who unrelentingly demanded honesty of himself, yet never asked his friends to be anything other than what they were.

Perhaps it can be said that there was a "habit of being" about him—as there was about Flannery O'Connor, another Catholic writer whom Merton much admired. Although intensely involved in his life as a monk of Gethsemani, his personal spiritual journey, Merton wanted to be equally involved in the lives of his friends. He yearned to know everything from Ernesto Cardenal about the Nicaraguan countryside and people; from Jim Forest, what life was like at the *Catholic Worker;* from Bob Lax, about the Greek icons; about James Laughlin's New Directions writers and poets, about children and grandchildren, about loves lost and found.

And while many people came to him for advice and counsel on the spiritual or worldly problems they were facing, Thomas Merton was not a man to readily offer advice, to attempt to "solve" something. (He saw himself as neither wise enough nor sufficiently of the spirit to be able to do that.) Usually he asked questions—and not about anything the person had come to discuss. He was very bad at mouthing dogma, never proselytized, and, as his friends related, rarely condemned or judged what they were already doing as "wrong." At times his behavior was frustrating to his friends; Merton didn't seem to be addressing exactly what they had come to him about. Yet, often a day, a year, even ten years later, they realized that Merton had indeed understood on a profoundly deep level and that, as filtered through his fine mind and a soul cleansed and purified by years of study and contemplation, he had offered insights they themselves had failed to comprehend at the time.

And even within the silent monastery cloister, although Father Louis was usually polite toward his fellow Trappists, reserving a curtly dismissive side for those he felt were wasting his time or who, with glazed eyes, were too eager to become Merton disciples, he had his special friends: monks he felt close to, with whom he could share more of himself. Merton absolutely needed people, even there. Not in the homogeneous, often lukewarm way encouraged in the days before Vatican II, but in real, intimate terms. Interestingly, his closest monk friends were not always the most articulate or intellectual. He sought in them what people surely saw in him—a certain integrity, an eagerness to know, a charity that accepted, embraced, and forgave human inconsistencies.

Although Merton hungered for real friendship, as he grew and deepened as a monk he began to resent the "social life" in the monastery: the sometimes almost promiscuous use of sign language (he was often a prime offender himself!), the constant activity involved in going to and from the abbey church six times a day, the rigorous work schedule. The very activities that break up the sometimes crushing boredom of monastic life slowly became burdensome to Merton. Orphaned at fifteen, this man at first loved being swallowed up in corporate activities. Over the years however, he became enervated by them. When finally, three years before he was to die, he was allowed to reside as a hermit on the Gethsemani grounds, Thomas Merton was overjoyed to finally live in solitude. It was a new opportunity for a new Thomas Merton to engage in a new intensity with his own depths, with his God. (But soon, being the old Thomas Merton, he was also engaged with the stream of friends who found their way to the rusty gate on Route 247 and up the rutted cart path to his door.)

The reflections of these twenty friends of Thomas Merton came about in a rather interesting way, one that was not anticipated. In the production of the Public Broadcasting Service documentary, *Merton,* a film crew and I set out to visit every important place Merton had ever been and to talk with people who knew him best, regardless of where they were. Such a comprehensive look at Merton had never before been attempted, and no one had personally interviewed his wide range of friends, scattered around the world. But at the Merton Project (the production company for the film) we felt that anything less would be a disservice to a man many of us had admired for so many years. (I too had been touched by *The Seven Storey Mountain* and, as a high school student, made a retreat at Gethsemani in 1956. In the ensuing years, as Merton's books came out I bought them, barely being able to read as quickly as he could write them.)

With 50,000 miles of travel behind us, and the film nearing the completion of six months of editing, I reread the interviews for a final check. I found myself alternately saddened that so little of what his friends had said about Thomas Merton eventually got into the documentary, and taken by the fascinating portrait that emerged. Obviously, this rich material needed to be brought together to serve as a unique, straightforward, unvarnished primer on a man about whom so much has been written, whose various aspects have been so closely studied that Merton as a human being often was neglected.

In this book, we meet twenty people who knew Merton at different phases in his life, for various lengths of time, and for many reasons. Some knew and saw him for decades; others corresponded with him for years but only saw him once or twice. I thought it would be interesting to have both the reflections of those who knew him over the years as well as the reflections of those who could bring the freshness that comes with limited contact.

The span reaches from George Linières in Montauban, France, who remembers an eight-year-old boy in knickerbockers, to His Holiness the Dalai Lama in Dharmsala, India, who, just weeks before Merton died, joked about the Trappist's fine, wide leather belt but at the same time sensed deeply that an important link between West and East had been forged. From the monks who saw his mood swings, personal struggles, and growth in the daily monastic life, to his dear friend, in whom he could confide that he was merely a man with a man's need for a woman. These are among the many views of Merton, in the words of those who knew him best.

PAUL WILKES

Hardwick, Massachusetts
March 1984

Acknowledgments

Special thanks go to Kristina Borjesson, the Merton Project's production manager and research director, to Tracy Wilkes for their faultless and patient transcription of the *Merton* interviews, and to Louise Fisher, who typed the manuscript. Thanks also go to the Merton Center for Religious Studies at Columbia University, under whose auspices and roof the film was produced and this book written, and to the funders of the PBS documentary *Merton,* most especially to the Catholic Communication Campaign, which gave a substantial grant early in the project asking not for editorial control, but just for a good film. Finally, thanks go to the men and women who appear on these pages. They had a good friend, and they have been generous enough to share him with the rest of us.

Thomas Merton:
An Introductory Sketch

Thomas Merton was born in Prades, France, in 1915. He spent roughly half his fifty-three years in the secular world, the other half as a cloistered Trappist monk at the Abbey of Our Lady of Gethsemani near Bardstown, Kentucky. He died of an accidental electrocution in Bangkok, Thailand, in 1968; it occurred during his first lengthy trip outside the monastery in twenty-seven years.

His early days in France and New York, at Cambridge and Columbia universities, were marked by an unquenchable thirst for experience, intellectual stimulation, pleasure, and also for meaning —the one quality of life that seemed to elude him as he indulged his other desires. In 1938, at Columbia University, Merton converted to Catholicism, and then, shocking many of his friends, joined the austere, silent Trappists in 1941.

The radical change in scene and lifestyle seemed to suit him. His first major book, *The Seven Storey Mountain,* published in 1948, detailed his early life, conversion, and first years at Gethsemani. It was a stunning literary, commercial, and inspirational success. The book was on the best-seller list for many months and to date has sold over three million copies. It has been published in fifteen languages.

Merton went on to write some sixty books, ranging from *New Seeds of Contemplation* (a spiritual classic not unlike the *Confessions of St. Augustine* or Thomas à Kempis's *Imitation of Christ*) to *Zen and the Birds of Appetite,* a description of his own growing attraction to and understanding of Eastern spiritual thought.

He wrote poetry, essays, reviews, meditations, history and autobiography; he was a photographer and a calligrapher. His output was prodigious, and his impact on the world outside the monastery was enormous. As his own thought and life progressed, he brought to his many readers and to the stream of visitors to Gethsemani an appreciation of contemplation, meditation, and the Christian religious quest. Once he was again aware of the pains and struggles of the world outside, he wrote forthrightly about the antiwar and civil rights movements, the nuclear arms buildup, and the crucial need for peace and justice in the modern world. In his later years his growing affinity for the East—at first a scandal within the Catholic Church—presaged the closer ties and interdisciplinary study so common today.

I. MERTON THE WRITER

James Laughlin

Laughlin is a fundamentally simple person. He is basically religious because he is *mundo corde,* clean of heart. I suppose that the last thing in the world that would occur to the superficial observer would be that the publisher of Henry Miller and others was "pure of heart." —*The Sign of Jonas*

James Laughlin knew Merton first as a poet, then as a prose writer —but always as a good friend. As the publisher of New Direc- tions, *he was involved with twelve of Merton's books, particularly the posthumous* Asian Journal, *which he assembled from Merton's notes. He was named by Merton to serve as one of the three trustees who oversee the Merton Legacy Trust, which has responsibility for Merton's literary estate.*

He was a wonderful friend. He loved people, and he could bring them out; he enjoyed bringing them out. Thomas Merton transformed many souls with his writing, but he wasn't a man to lecture or proselytize. I felt he was interested in me, as a poet, a publisher, a person—not as a lost sheep. I surely wasn't alone; the files at the Merton Center at Bellarmine College show that he corresponded with several thousand people.

I loved to go down to Gethsemani to visit him at the monastery because, very simply, we had such good times. I would pick up a car at the Louisville Airport and drive down to the monastery. "Pax Intrantibus," (Peace to those who enter) it says over the gate. Father Abbot always gave Tom permission to go off with me for the day. Tom would start out circumspectly—he would go to the storage room for an old bishop's suit and exit from the monastery looking very ecclesiastical, so as not to shock the gate brother. A few miles, and he'd say "Stop here." He would go into the woods, take off his bishop's suit, put on his blue jeans, his old sweater, and his beret, and get back into the car with a sigh of relief. Then we would head east, stopping, I must confess, at a few rural beer parlors along the way; Tom was always very popular with the local farmers. He knew how to talk to all kinds of people; they found him funny and they liked him. Often we'd head on over to Lexington for lunch with his wonderful friends, the great old Austrian painter and printer, Victor Hammer. Carolyn Hammer put on superb gourmet lunches for us, and there was always an excellent bottle (or two) of wine, which Tom and I would down with relish, he never showing any effect. It was curious—he had no allergy whatsoever to alcohol.

Later in his life he became even more relaxed, but right from the beginning of our friendship there was something wonderful and alive in him that even the Trappist life couldn't suppress.

My first contact with Tom, back in the early 1940s, came through Mark Van Doren. Mark was one of the greatest teachers of literature we have ever had in this country. He was Tom's mentor at Columbia.

When Mark, for whom I had published some poems at New Directions, told me he had received thirty poems from a very promising young poet, one with deep spiritual feeling and one whom he thought I would probably not find out about in the normal course of business, I was interested. I liked those early poems very much. There was a freshness there, a liveliness, a verbal spriteliness that was attractive. They were not like anything that any of the other New Directions poets were writing. There was an almost ingenuous character to them, which was appealing.

The Catholic message in those early poems was strong. I mean, there were poems about the night the monastery barn burned up and the portrait of the Virgin in the cloister . . . At first, such subjects didn't interest me too much. What I liked was Merton's imagery and the way he could take a religious subject and carry it into real-life metaphors, so that I, as a heretic, a benighted Calvinist, was able to get some feeling, as I never had before, of what the Catholic faith was about.

At that time this was the only kind of poetry that the abbot wanted Fr. Louis to write. As religious poetry, it didn't come close to George Herbert or Hopkins; yet those poems have passionate, authentic feeling for what he is writing about. The finest of *Thirty Poems* is the poem written in memory of his brother, John Paul, who was killed in the war. This is a very beautiful, very moving poem by anyone's standard. Just to quote a few lines:

FOR MY BROTHER:
REPORTED MISSING IN ACTION, 1943

Sweet brother, if I do not sleep
My eyes are flowers for your tomb;
And if I cannot eat my bread,
My fasts shall live like willows where you died.
If in the heat I find no water for my thirst,
My thirst shall turn to springs for you, poor traveller.

As Merton matured in the 1950s and 1960s, becoming more secular in his interests, he began to write a different kind of poetry, which was more concerned with what was happening outside the monastery, and inside himself.

I'll never forget my first trip to Gethsemani. It was after New Directions had published *Thirty Poems*. Tom and I had corresponded, talking about other books that he might write, and the abbot invited me to visit him. This was a very novel experience for me, going to stay in a monastery—which, if I accepted the prejudices of my Presbyterian mother, I would have considered an invention of the devil himself. Of course, it wasn't at all. It turned out to be a place full of happiness and high spirits. I had expected to meet a somber-faced monk, such as you saw in old etchings, pacing silently in the cloister, muttering prayers under his breath. Tom wasn't like that at all! From the moment I was greeted by a smiling gate brother, I saw that I had been completely misinformed about monasteries; this was a joyous place, and Tom Merton was joyous. For me, he had, in the old sense of the word, *gaiety;* he had a wonderful gaiety, about his vocation and about life.

Tom wasn't the handsomest man but he had a wonderful smile,

a lovely laugh, and he was smiling most of the time. He was charismatic and empathetic; he put himself immediately in touch with me. Immediately he was asking me all sorts of questions: what was I writing? did I have any new poems with me? what was my family background? what books was New Directions publishing? Tom was interested in everything; there was practically no subject he didn't want to know about. He was bubbling with enthusiasm. One problem, of course, occasionally, was that he bubbled so much, though not in any stupid or foolish way. He would arrive at dawn at the guesthouse, when I was struggling to get my eyes open, with a green sack full of books and notes, things he had thought of during the night—did he sleep at all?—that he wanted to discuss with me. And this would go on all day.

He was a man churning with ideas who constantly asked himself if those ideas stacked up. And that is the sign of a writer and a thinker who is constantly growing. And grow he certainly did, from the early days of *The Seven Storey Mountain* to later writings, which, as the French would say, were *"au point."*

The Seven Storey Mountain was a great best-seller because it had things to say that people—and not just Catholics—were, at that moment in our social history, waiting to hear. It was 1948, and the book presented an answer to spiritual problems that many were confronting—particularly the young, who were upset by the way things were going in the country, by the threat of an atomic holocaust, and all the rest of it. Merton voiced their concerns, so simply and directly. He was responding in his personal terms to a general angst.

One might say that *The Seven Storey Mountain* is in some respects slightly undisciplined, perhaps even preachy at times. But in his later books, particularly in the journals, Tom controlled himself more and held to the track. He also gained greatly in writing style. Merton was a natural, born writer. He understood the possibilities of language. And he got better and better as he went along.

Once you've been bitten by Merton, you will continue to read him, and read everything you can. How he actually did it, who knows? Can any of us really analyze the particular magic of a great? Something was combusting inside Tom, and it came out in fine language, clear thought, persuasive communication. He touched people's minds and hearts.

I think the books (still unpublished) that really give both an insight into his writing and his search are Tom's private journals. He was a prodigious worker, and a very fast writer, and when I visited him I saw that he was working on two sets of journals. One set was the journals that he soon made into books. The other was the private journals, which he kept in big black ledgers. These were his very personal thoughts, like a diary, written just for his own dialogue with himself. The quality of them was very free, very frank; quite often he was talking to God, asking advice from God. Often he was worrying about whether he was a good contemplative, whether he was indulging egotism in writing worldly books; seeking from God enlightenment on why he had never had a major mystical experience. He directed us, his trustees, that these journals should not be published until twenty-five years after his death.

I know Tom sought to lose his identity in the great nothingness, "to drown in the sea of the infinite," as Leopardi put it. That is what every contemplative seeks. But he was humble; he knew the literature of mysticism and knew that this is something you can't reach out and take. He knew his place, his need for grace.

If you read the end of Merton's *Asian Journal*—when he got to Polonnaruwa in Ceylon—I think you will be convinced, as I was, that he finally had his great mystical experience there. It's ironic that it was Buddhism, and the art of Buddhism, that brought him this long-sought experience, and not something in the monastery or in the Catholic faith. And to me it's appropriate that this vision came to him through his ecumenism. He would never have gone to Ceylon if he had not read Buddhist texts at the monastery. There at Polonnaruwa he looked at those sleeping Buddha figures in their massive tranquility, and knew that he had at last come to the place where time stopped. He was a part of the universal whole that is nothing. There was no more Thomas Merton, there was only the infinite compassion. This is how he reported the event:

I am able to approach the Buddhas barefoot and undisturbed, my feet in wet grass, wet sand. Then the silence of the extraordinary faces. The great smiles. Huge and yet subtle. Filled with every possibility, questioning nothing, the peace not of emotional resignation but of Madhyamika, of sunyata, that has seen through every question without trying to discredit anyone or anything—*without refutation*—without establishing some other argument. For the doctrinaire, the mind that needs well-established positions, such peace, such silence, can be frightening. I was knocked over with a rush of relief and thankfulness at the *obvious* clarity of the figures, the clarity and fluidity of shape and line, the design of the monumental bodies composed into the rock shape and landscape, figure, rock and tree. And the sweep of bare rock sloping away on the other side of the hollow, where you can go back and see different aspects of the figure.

Looking at these figures I was suddenly, almost forcibly, jerked clean out of the habitual, half-tied vision of things and an inner clearness, clarity, as if exploding from the rocks themselves, became evident and obvious. . . . All problems are resolved and everything is clear, simply because what matters is clear. The rock, all matter, all life, is charged with dharmakaya . . . everything is emptiness and everything is compassion. I don't know when in my life I have ever had such a sense of beauty and spiritual validity running together in one aesthetic illumination. Surely, with Mahabalipuram [near Madras] and Polonnaruwa, my Asian pilgrimage has come clear and purified itself.

I mean, I know and have seen what I was obscurely looking for. I don't know what else remains but I have now seen and have pierced through the surface and have got beyond the shadow and the disguise. *The Asian Journal of Thomas Merton,* 1975, pp. 233–236

In the ten or fifteen years before his death, there was a definite change in the inner climate of Merton's life. When he first came to the monastery in 1941, he had all the proper attitudes of a postulant, then those of a novice, then those of a young priest. He was humble, he was obedient, he fully believed that whatever the abbot said was what he should do. But later, as he matured, had his success, and realized his power as a writer, his perception of his

role began to change. I think that in the response to *The Seven
Storey Mountain* he sensed the element of sensational publicity, perhaps little more. You know, "Wicked young man runs off to
monastery to save soul." But, with his other books, he saw what
he could do with his writing, and this gave him more confidence
to be himself. He grew less willing to accept the restrictions demanded by some bishop writing to the abbot to tell him what Fr.
Louis might and might not write. Was this vanity, or arrogance?
No, because Tom was always mindful of working for God. He
was a monk; he would serve. But he altered his interpretations of
what God wanted him, as a writer, to do. This comes through
very clearly in Michael Mott's biography of Merton. With much
detail of actual quotations, working from the journals, Mott traces
the stages of Merton's revisions of his attitudes toward the Deity,
the Church, and the responsibilities of a monk.

There were frequent debates with the abbot when Tom began
to write about social conditions, civil rights, and more when he
became involved—even became a leader—for liberal Catholics in
the movement. Friction with the abbot increased when his opposition to the Vietnam War led to articles attacking the Pentagon or
the President. The more conservative Catholic bishops bore down
on the abbot: "You must restrain this monk. All he's supposed to
do is pray; he has no business concerning himself with social
movements and the Vietnam War." Tom often let off steam to me
about this repression in his letters, and naturally I sided with him,
though I liked and admired Dom James.

On my next visit to Gethsemani, I accosted Dom James as he
was coming across the west field. His robes were blowing in the
wind and he looked very handsome and beautiful—like a figure in
a Winslow Homer painting.

"Father Abbot, can I have a word?"

"Certainly, James."

"Father, I think God wants Father Louis to go on being *slightly*
political." (I underscored the *slightly*.)

Dom James said to me, "James, try to understand. Fr. Louis's
work and the work of all us monks is to pray; our prayers will rise

up to Heaven and God will hear them, and God will solve the problems of the world.''

Well, I was polite, and I didn't say the short word that popped into my mind.

I just said "Thank you, Father."

I understood that Dom James was trying to run the monastery by the Rule of St. Benedict and that he honestly believed it was best for Tom's soul to submit to obedience. Tom, with his spirit and his gift with words, was not an easy monk to "handle." When we talked about Dom James, it came through to me that Tom, in a certain way, relished the arguments with his superior and even, in a stranger way, *needed* them. He sounded off to his friends about Dom James in letters, but there was, I'm convinced, deep love and respect between these two strong-willed men who were so different in temperament. Dom James, beyond his abbatial duty, cared for Fr. Louis; he chose him to be his personal confessor.

The bishops kept up the pressure, and Tom finally agreed that he would stop publishing his political writing. But he set up a private publishing system for them; it reminded me of the Russian *samizdat* network. And there are a whole series of polemical writings that Tom called the "Cold War Letters." Tom wrote these pieces, got young friends in the novitiate to mimeograph them, and then (through friends such as "Ping" Ferry) had them sent to an ever-growing mailing list. Thus the "Cold War Letters" had an influential circulation. They were quoted and passed from hand to hand.

We also see a profound change in Merton's poetry about 1963 when his book *Emblems of a Season of Fury* was published. This was the first time he felt he could write secular poetry about social and political themes and get away with it. Here was a superb poem called "Chant to Be Used in Processions Around a Site with Furnaces." This is about the German concentration camps of the Holocaust. It is done with a wonderful kind of ingenuous irony, such as he later uses in "Original Child Bomb," his dead-pan account of the Hiroshima bomb. In "[Chant to Be Used in Processions,"] Merton uses Pound's "persona" mask technique, where he speaks through the mouth of one of the Nazi executioners. The irony is devastating when the SS officer urges the prisoners in the camp to write home to their friends to invite them to come to their "joke." This kind of black humor crops up continually in his later work.*

The poetry of Merton that I find the greatest, the most liberated from convention, and the most extraordinary is the first book of his long poem, *The Geography of Lograire*. This was planned to be his "work in progress," his *Cantos,* his "Paterson." He told me he expected to be working on it for the rest of his life.

The "geography" of the poem simply is that of Merton's mind. He intended to make a personal epic of everything that had gone on in the geography of his mind, everything he had read, everything he remembered, but all distilled into compact, almost symbolic short poems. He only completed one volume of *Lograire,* which he left with me before he went to Asia and said, "If anything happens to me, I want you to publish this." I composed the necessary notes on his sources and brought it out about a year after his death.

Tom had read widely in history, in anthropology and in many other areas. Few such books were in the monastery library, but Carolyn Hammer found them for him at the University of Kentucky. But *Lograire* is not simply pastiche or a potpourri. What matters is what he could do with such diverse materials. From history he fashioned myths about the English Ranters and the Dakota Indian "Ghost Dances." From anthropology he made his own myths, such as those about the Cargo Cults in Micronesia. Blending language from ads in the *New Yorker,* with Covarrubras's accounts of the early Mexican Indians, he made delicious parodies of female fashions. Where he got copies of the *New Yorker,* I'll never know, but he did.

Merton had an acute sense of humor, which is seen in his poem "Chee$e." This makes fun of the Trappist cheese business at the monastery, of which Tom was always scornful; it parodies Joyce

---

* Editor's note: This poem is partially quoted on p. 30 of this book, by Lawrence Ferlinghetti

Kilmer's poem "Trees." There's a nice touch when he spells it
chee$e.

CHEE$E
Joyce Killer-Diller

I think that we should never freeze
Such lively assets as our cheese:

The sucker's hungry mouth is pressed
Against the cheese's caraway breast

A cheese, whose scent like sweet perfume
Pervades the house through every room.

A cheese that may at Christmas wear
A suit of cellophane underwear,

Upon whose bosom is a label,
Whose habitat:—The Tower of Babel.

Poems are nought but warmed-up breeze,
Dollars are made by Trappist Cheese.

—*The Collected Poems of
Thomas Merton* (1980), pp. 799–800

During these years when he was maturing, Tom did grouse a
good deal about restrictions at the monastery. He disliked the
cheese business and the junky stuff in the shop that sold little
crucifixes or rosaries to the tourists. Once I asked, "Well, Tom,
why, if it gives you this much pain, why do you stay there? After
all, you're a brilliant writer, you could go out in the world. You
could still do your spiritual teaching, you'd be a very successful
writer. Why do you stay there?" He looked at me incredulously
and said, "J., you don't understand. That's where I belong. That's
my home."

Until he was given his hermitage up in the woods, he complained about conversation in the monastery. We think that Trappist monks don't talk, but that isn't necessarily so. They may talk
as much as they want with their hands, in sign language. This
irritated Tom and may have been a reason why he longed for the

life of a hermit. Of course, I found a curious contradiction there, that this man who loved people and was in touch with so many of them all over the world wanted to isolate himself. Yet some of his most beautiful prose is about the solitary life and the concept of solitude. His translations of the writings of the Desert Fathers reflect this concern. It is a theme that recurs in so many of his later books.

At one point he was corresponding with a bishop in Cuernavaca about the possibility of living in a cave and administering to the poor Indians. If he had actually done that, how much would he have missed those interesting intellectual visits from Catholic thinkers such as Jacques Maritain and the writers from everywhere who came to see him. And I don't think he would have stuck it out very long as a hermit in Mexico or Alaska, away from Gethsemani, which was the only home he ever really knew.

Robert Giroux

The Seven Storey Mountain has been rejected by one of the Censors of the Order: not on theological grounds, but as unripe for publication. . . . I am held to be incapable of writing an autobiography "with his present literary equipment" and I am advised to take a correspondence course in English grammar. ———*The Sign of Jonas*

Robert Giroux, Columbia 1936, graduated from college with honors and was elected to Phi Beta Kappa. After three years at CBS, he entered publishing at the end of 1939 and became editor-in-chief at Harcourt, Brace & Company. In 1955 he joined the house—Farrar, Straus & Giroux—that has borne his name since 1964. In addition to working with and publishing some of the most noted writers of our time, he is himself a writer. His study of Shakespeare's sonnets, The Book Known as Q *(1982), is now a Vintage paperback. He has written introductions for Flannery O'Connor's* Complete Stories, *John Berryman's* The Freedom of the Poet, *and Elizabeth Bishop's* Collected Prose. *He has published memoirs of Jean Stafford and T. S. Eliot, and he gave the Bowker Lecture, "The Education of an Editor," in 1982.*

Could you tell us about the Columbia College of that period? It seems to have been a heady time, an era of intellectual ferment. What was it like when Thomas Merton arrived on the scene?

I was in the class of 1936, one year ahead of Merton—and a whole year makes a big difference in college. In the 1930s the country was still in the midst of the Depression; the times were serious, and most students seemed to be serious about their goals. There were a lot of interesting undergraduates at Columbia College then, like John Latouche, who became famous in the musical theater; Ad Rinehardt, who became a famous painter; Herman

Wouk, who became a famous writer; John Berryman, who became one of our best poets; James Weschler, Leonard Robinson, Robert Lax, Robert Paul Smith, Ed Rice, Ernest Kroll, Robert Gibney, and many more—they all made their mark as writers or in the arts. Thomas Merton had come to Columbia from England; the first thing I noticed was his British accent, which he quickly lost. He seemed to be better educated, and much more widely read, than most of my classmates; his years at Clare College, Cambridge, had left their mark. Like the rest of this group, Tom naturally gravitated toward the classes taught by Mark Van Doren. I also heard he was interested in *Jester,* the undergraduate humor magazine, for which he was drawing cartoons.

When did your first meeting with Merton occur?

I was editor of the literary magazine, the *Columbia Review,* with offices on the fourth floor of John Jay Hall. This blond, stocky young man walked in and introduced himself as Tom Merton. We talked a bit and I found that he was interested in jazz, Harlem, and the movies—especially the films of W. C. Fields, the Marx Brothers, Charlie Chaplin, and Preston Sturges, enthusiasms I shared. This was in 1935. He said he had written something for us. It was a documentary piece, inspired by something he'd witnessed a couple of days before—an accident that had shocked him very much because it resulted in a death. I remember one image, a pack of cigarettes in a pool of blood. And one of the key words was *meaningless.* I thought, "This man is a good writer, he has an eye for detail, for the apt image." But the piece was too long, verbose, and overwritten. I cut it, and he was a bit upset and protested. I said, "No, Tom, what remains is really the best part and we'll print it." I became his editor at that point, you see. This was one of his first published pieces, I think, unless he had published at Cambridge.

Politics were important in those days, but what about religion?

Religion was a subject that was never discussed or mentioned. For example, I don't remember the words *religion* or *Catholic* or

Christian or *theology* ever being used while I was on the campus. It was something private and personal. I can't recall any religious discussions. I knew that Father Ford was the Catholic chaplain, but I didn't meet him until long after I graduated, until in fact I published Merton. And Tom's conversion and decision to become a Trappist in 1941 were a great surprise. I had no idea whatever that he was remotely interested in religion.

Tell us about the early manuscripts he sent when you were a Harcourt editor.

After I graduated from Columbia (and of course Tom stayed on for his senior year), I lost touch with him completely. I worked at CBS a couple of years and then I joined Harcourt, Brace's editorial staff late in 1939. In February 1940 Merton submitted—not to me, but to the firm—a novel entitled *The Straits of Dover*. It came to my desk and at first I did not recognize the name, Thomas James Merton. As I read, I realized who it was. My report called it "a strange novel, which seems to be concerned with lots of people, but has no particular plot. The central figure is a boy who attended school in England, went to Cambridge briefly, and ended up at Columbia. It also features a stupid millionaire, a showgirl who is after him, a left-wing intellectual, a Hindu mystic, etc. I think Mr. Merton has writing ability, but this wobbles around, and gets nowhere." I wrote Tom an encouraging rejection.

Only two months later another novel, *The Labyrinth,* came in. I saw that it was an improved and tightened version of *The Straits of Dover,* but at the end the young man from Columbia was still floundering around in his labyrinth and the story was without a resolution. I sent him a note: "Dear Tom, As I told you on the phone, the vote was negative. But all the editors agree with me that we should see anything you may do. I'm sorry this is not the one to launch you with. Let me hear from you again when you return from Cuba."

In April 1941 my good friend Naomi Burton, the literary agent, sent me Tom's third novel. *The Man in the Sycamore Tree.* It still wasn't right, and I sent it back. The last communication I had from Merton before he became a Trappist was dated October 1, 1941. He asked me to read *The Journal of My Escape from the Nazis*. At that stage (Europe was already at war) this imaginary journal was even more impossible to publish than the earlier books. He has described it in *The Seven Storey Mountain* as follows: "It fulfilled a kind of psychological necessity that had been pent up in me all through the last stages of the war, because of my sense of identification and my guilt with what was going on in England. . . . The book got away up more than one blind alley." We rejected it, and it was published many years later with Naomi's introduction.

Did you meet him after college, before he joined the Trappists?

In the summer of 1941 (he joined the monastery late that year), I encountered him on Fifth Avenue, of all places—in Scribner's Bookstore, one of the best bookstores in New York. He touched me on the arm, and I turned around and there was Tom Merton. I said, "Tom, what are you doing these days? I hope you're still writing." He said, "Well, I've just been to the *New Yorker* to see Bob Gerdy"—another classmate of ours who was on the staff of the magazine. I asked, "Are you going to write for the *New Yorker?*" He said that they wanted him to write about Gethsemani, and when I asked what it was, he replied, "It's a Trappist monastery in Kentucky, where I've been making retreats." I was stunned; this was an absolute revelation. He said, "Yes, Gerdy wants me to write about it." When I said it sounded fascinating, he replied, "But I couldn't think of writing about it." That told me everything. His true character was now clear. I wished him well, and we parted. I next heard about him from Mark Van Doren, who phoned to say, "Tom Merton has become a Trappist monk." Again I was stunned, but less so this time. Mark Van Doren said, "We'll never hear from him again. He's taken a vow of silence, he can't write to us nor we to him—he's leaving the world. I think he's an extraordinary young man, and I don't believe we'll ever hear another word from him." Mark said that Tom had left him his manuscript of thirty poems, which he was sending to Jay

Laughlin at New Directions, who published it. Little did we know what other books would follow.

Did you think his vocation was going to last?

The monastery? I think I did, yes. I really knew nothing about the monastic life. I thought it would be a hard life, ascetic, severe, cut off from everything. And I knew Tom was a communicator, a person who was very good with words, a writer. How would he fit his talent and ability to communicate into an isolated and cut-off kind of life? That was Mark Doren's concern too. We both thought of him as an artist, you see, which he was. As it turned out, the abbot who was then presiding at Gethsemani, Abbot Frederic Dunne, must have been a very wise man. It is he who ordered Merton to write his life story. Tom told me he did not really want to write *The Seven Storey Mountain*. He was obliged to write it. He was given an office and a typewriter, and he resisted, thinking, "I've left behind my past life to come here." Yet he was made to relive it. So in a way Abbot Dunne solved the problem Mark Van Doren and I had perceived. And the great success of the book embarrassed Thomas Merton. Of course he was widely criticized for writing it, not only by reviewers but by other religious who said he'd taken the vow of silence. Even I, as his publisher, got hate mail, letters saying things like "Why don't you shut up this talking Trappist?" I had a standard reply: "Writing is a form of contemplation."

Did you hear from Merton at all before you received the manuscript of The Seven Storey Mountain?

No, not at all. It was not until December 1946 that Naomi Burton sent me the manuscript with a note that said, "Brother Louis has asked me to send you this." At that point I did not know that Brother Louis was his monastic name. I phoned Naomi and wired him our acceptance two days before Christmas.

Did the book require a great deal of editing?

As I recall, the editing was fairly minimal. This was almost forty years ago, remember. I did some cutting, and I believe I chose the marvelous opening paragraph, which was not how it began originally. But my cutting was nothing in comparison to Evelyn Waugh's. He later edited the British edition, which he retitled *Elected Silence,* a phrase from Gerard Manley Hopkins, and he cut nearly one-third more than I; he even cut out Tom's poem to his brother killed in the war. Of course before I saw the manuscript, the monastic censors had deleted a great many passages they thought might "give scandal." I've often wondered what they would have done to St. Augustine's *Confessions.*

What was your initial response to the manuscript?

I was quite excited about it and took it to Donald Brace, my boss at the time. The head of the trade department—Frank Morley, on whom I relied greatly for editorial advice—had just left. I told Mr. Brace it was a manuscript by a former classmate of mine, an autobiography about his conversion to Catholicism and his decision to enter a Trappist monastery. "You really like it?" he asked and I said, "Yes, very much. Why don't you read it, Mr. Brace?" Instead he merely asked whether I thought it would lose any money. I told him I really didn't think we'd lose any money, but whether we'd make any was problematic. It seemed to be a strong book, and I felt that the timing was right. This was the post war period, with a feeling of great disillusionment. Everything should have been changed by the awful war, but it became pretty clear by 1947 that nothing at all was changing, in fact it was going to start all over again. But now I had Mr. Brace's tacit blessing, and we did contract for the book.

Did you at any time think you were about to publish a best-seller?

No, when the book was published on October 4, 1948, it did not seem to me, nor to anyone else in the firm, that it would become a national phenomenon. It merely looked as if the book would "do all right." Its prepublication sale was 20,847 copies, which is very good indeed. Our expectations had been modest. We contemplated a first printing of 5,000 copies, which was later increased by 20,000. After publication the book in its first month sold only 5,914 additional copies and by the end of the year, when critics were choosing the "Outstanding Books of 1948," *The Seven Storey Mountain* wasn't even mentioned. Not once—not even under that most condescending of headings, "Religious Books." But meanwhile something was happening: readers were discovering the book for themselves and we had to reprint several times. The sales, which in November had gone up another 12,957 copies, had in December suddenly shot up by 31,000 copies. That last figure is particularly significant. In the book trade it is usual for fewer orders to be received in December than in any other month. (It's important to remember that these are *publisher's* orders, not the bookstore sales.) Christmas orders have nearly all been filled by the end of November; if bookstores haven't sold the books by closing time December 24th, they are likely to be inventoried right back to the publisher in January. Yet between Christmas and New Year's the order clerks of Harcourt, Brace had one of their busiest periods in the entire year. New readers, all over the country, averaging *two thousand* every business day, wanted the book out of season, for its own sake, and they wanted it in extraordinary quantities. The process continued during 1949. In May of that year, when I visited Thomas Merton at Gethsemani, I presented him with Copy No. 100,000. In the original cloth edition, the trade sale exceeded 600,000 copies.

Tell us about those famous advance quotes.

Yes, early in 1948—long before publication—I sent galley proofs to three famous people, asking them for quotes and wondering if anyone would respond. They not only all replied, but they used extraordinary terms. Evelyn Waugh: "It should take its place among the classic records of spiritual experience." Graham Greene called it "an autobiography with a pattern and meaning valid for all of us." Clare Boothe Luce predicted that in one hundred years readers "will turn to this book to find out what went on in the heart of a man in this cruel century." It was at this point that we first decided to increase the prepublication printing order;

it went up again during the summer, after three book clubs made it their major fall selection. I remember the first review, by Ann Wolfe in the *Saturday Review,* which said that "It stands as a more human document than the comparable *Apologia Pro Sua Vita* of John Henry Newman." Dr. Connolly of Fordham wrote me that it "combines some of the best elements of Newman's *Apologia,* Gerard Manley Hopkins' *Notebooks,* and Johannes Jorgensen's *Autobiography."* Msgr. Fulton Sheen called it "a Twentieth Century form of the *Confessions* of St. Augustine."

What was your impression the first time you went to Gethsemani to see Merton?

It was the occasion of his ordination to the priesthood. A group of his friends was invited by Abbot James Fox to visit the monastery. And I brought along with me the 100,000th copy off the press, done in a special morocco binding as a presentation copy for Tom, which he seemed pleased to have. But the abbey was a new experience for me. I was impressed by the simplicity of the place. All the monks were very direct, and their reactions were simple and open. It was a happy place, and a very hard-working place. Far from the perfect peace and quiet you expected, you heard the rattle of farm machinery all day. The serenity was interior. They sang psalms at intervals all day long, starting at two in the morning at Matins, when their day began. They retired at sunset—a healthy farmer's life.

How about Merton, had he changed?

He looked happier to me, more put-together. He was thinner, in his white habit. For work he wore a black apron or tunic over the habit, which was removed when they sang the office. It seemed to me that he'd found his metier. He was in the right place.

You said that Merton wouldn't write about Gethsemani for a magazine, and yet he became the most public of private men.

This was a paradox that worried him, and he often wondered whether he should be publishing books at all. He was very sensitive to criticism from fellow monks, fellow religious, and laity too. The other paradox was that he found himself to be in touch with more people after he got to Gethsemani than he'd ever been in his life. It was due to his books. He had correspondence with Boris Pasternak in Russia, with Dr. Suzuki the Zen Buddhist in Japan, and with leading theologians and writers all over the world. His letters should be published. Tom's other language, of course, was French. Once when I was at the abbey he was assigned as the interpreter for the abbot general. The Trappist Cistercian order originated in France, and the general was a Frenchman who did not speak a word of English. Tom not only wrote in French, but spoke fluent French. After all, he was born in France and had his early schooling there.

What would you say happened to Thomas Merton over the years?

He grew up fast, like Huckleberry Finn. Of all the writers I've known—and I've known some very great ones, very complicated ones—no one had quite the speed of intellectual growth that Thomas Merton had. He just deepened and matured, and became more and more intense and marvelous as the years went by, in a way that is quite remarkable. This growth was implicit in him. Why does a particular plant develop so fast? Because it has the capacity to do so and is helped by its environment. He himself lived in the climate and in the atmosphere that fostered intellectual and spiritual growth. He had really found his vocation. I'm sometimes asked, "What would he have been like if he hadn't been a monk?" I don't know. He probably would have been good at almost anything he might have undertaken. But at the monastery he was able to mature and grow in the most remarkable way. It was absolutely the right soil, the right setting, the right place for him. It wasn't without its difficulties. One irony was that Merton did not receive a penny of his enormous royalties, which of course belonged to the community of monks and helped them to build daughter-houses elsewhere in the country. I remember that one such monastery in the West consisted at that time of a group of Quonset huts. But imagine yourself a writer, writing the best you can, and then turning in your manuscript to your fellow-monks who tell you what's wrong with it. This was before the publisher ever saw it, you understand. The censors went through it, and often they would pick out absurd points, all kinds of things that had nothing to do with writing but with—well, public relations. But Tom was good-natured and cheerful, and put up with it. He'd let off some steam in letters, saying, "They have to do it, I understand, it's part of my life here."

Do you know if any book of his was actually suppressed?

I do not think so. But one of his best books was *almost* suppressed—not by Gethsemani, whose censors had passed it, but by the French superiors. It was rescued at the last minute. The book in question was *The Sign of Jonas*. We had already set up the text when Tom ran into unexpected difficulties. The abbot, returning from an annual convocation in France, stopped off in New York to tell me that *The Sign of Jonas,* now in galley proofs, could not be published. The monastery would reimburse us for all our expenses, but the matter was beyond appeal. Guessing that something must have occurred in France, I asked whether the abbot general, who knew no English, had read the manuscript. No, I was told, publication had been forbidden on the grounds that a personal journal was not consonant with the traditions of the Trappist Order. This puzzled me, because his autobiography had already been published. I somehow felt that the seat of the trouble lay in the French language and French mentality, and asked Jacques Maritain, who admired Merton and was teaching at Princeton, to write to the abbot general asking him to reconsider. Maritain's letter, in elegant French, pointed out that St. Bernard of Clairvaux, the greatest Trappist, was famous as the author of books, including his meditations. *The Sign of Jonas* was released.

Some critics have regarded Merton's life as an odyssey, a search for a home. What do you think of this?

It may well be that this was Merton's psychology, and it has to do with the simple fact that he was an orphan. He lost his mother when a child, and he lost his father while still young. I've seen this in other writers. A writer whose posthumous prose I've been working with is the poet Elizabeth Bishop. I didn't fully understand her work until I found that her father died when she was eight months old, and her mother went into a mental institution as a result of the father's death. She traveled a great deal, you know, and one of her most famous books of poetry, *Questions of Travel,* has to do with the various places she lived. Some people would say that Merton found a home in the monastery. It may be true, but that doesn't take one iota away from his achievement. Many people have found homes in monasteries, but few have developed as remarkably as he did. The ambience never really explains the art itself. Two people with equal talent could be put in the same setting, but the results may not be the same. Art is a mystery. Why *X* happens instead of *Y,* nobody can tell.

What about his trip to the East at the end of his life?

I don't think he ever found a home, but I think he found happiness then. I never saw him in that period, but his friends say he seemed very happy in those last years. I don't think it was just because he was traveling and getting away from Kentucky. He was deeply interested in the religious thought of the East, in Zen Buddhism, in Asia in general. Going there was of great importance to him. He was also meeting his peers, men of intellectual capacities equal to his own. That was a source of great happiness for him. The fact that it was Asia was another plus, but these were simply stops along his pilgrim's road, wayside stations, but not the end of his existence. He died in Thailand, but it was simply another stop along the way.

Would you describe the day you found out that Merton had died?

Mark Van Doren called me. He was deeply shocked, and so was I. After all, Tom was relatively young. For a man at the height of his abilities, he had decades of work and writing and living to do, and so it was a tragedy from that point of view. But in hindsight it seems to have been an almost perfect life. He worked out a pattern and a meaning in his life that have given a great deal to other people. Surely he will remain in history as one of the most remarkable men of our time. What he had to say about the nonviolent method of dealing with the horrible problems we all face has appealed tremendously, particularly to young people. He simply has been a remarkable American, writer, poet, thinker, and monk. It's hard to think of anybody in the last few decades who achieved so much.

What would you say is the most misunderstood thing about Thomas Merton?

He certainly isn't a saint. I think he would be horrified to be spoken of in that way. If there is any resentment against or resistance to him, it probably is the religious aspect. I think most people are suspicious of religious figures, because their motivation can be so ambiguous. It's hard to know whether they mean to do you good, or are doing it for self-aggrandizement or self-interest.

But was he doing it for self-aggrandizement?

Not in the least. That I'm positive of. On the contrary, in his earlier years his realization that he was being pushed into a celebrity role was the last thing on earth he wanted. Yet one of the reasons for Merton's great appeal is that he was very much a man of his own times. Far from being limited by his seclusion in a monastery, he flourished. Young people everywhere responded to his sanity, his pacifism, and his intelligence. He believed in a nonviolent alternative to war, and was convinced that a knowledge of the past was a precondition for understanding the present: those who do not absorb the past remain children mentally. He considered the two greatest curses of modern life to be infantilism and illiteracy, the products of bad schooling and of the decay of American education. If high school and college graduates are illiterate or semiliterate, how can they absorb the past, let alone cope with the present? Merton always felt that youths, many of whom considered themselves highly sophisticated, who embraced the drug culture thinking it would mean freedom and release, were too infantile to perceive that drugs, far from providing an escape, are a trap. It may be that Thomas Merton's premature death on his first extended trip away from the monastery was a tragedy, but there is solace in the knowledge that his books continue to move steadily, winning new readers every year.

Lawrence Ferlinghetti

If you write for God you will reach many men and bring them joy.

If you write for men—you may make some money and you give someone a little joy and you may make a noise in the world, for a little while.

If you write only for yourself you can read what you yourself have written and after ten minutes you will be so disgusted you will wish that you were dead.   —*New Seeds of Contemplation*

Lawrence Ferlinghetti, sixty-three, is a poet, novelist, playwright, and an editor. He earned a Doctorat de L'Université at the Sorbonne in 1950. His City Lights, in San Francisco, was the first all-paperback bookstore in America. City Lights Books, of which he is editor, publishes modern poetry and prose. Among his many books, Coney Island of the Mind *is perhaps his best-known work, with nearly one million copies in print.*

I read *The Seven Storey Mountain* in the late 1940s at a time when I was reading a lot of Catholic literature: St. Augustine, the whole bunch. But Merton was probably the first modern Catholic writer that I had ever read. And inasmuch as I had gone to Columbia University in 1946–1947 I identified with him quite strongly. I was very involved in exploring Catholicism at that time, and the Trappist discipline intrigued me. But what made *Seven Storey Mountain* especially interesting to me was that here was this poet, this Columbia intellectual who was converted. Especially at a time when most poets were going the other way and becoming unconverted. Like Jack Kerouac, who went from Catholicism to Buddhism.

Then I had no contact with him until, in 1961, at City Lights Books, we were ready to publish *Journal for the Protection of All Beings*. We asked a lot of nonpolitical writers and thinkers and poets and artists to make a statement on the state of the world at that time. Merton wrote back with this long prose poem, "Chant to Be Used in Procession Around a Site with Furnaces."

We were very honored and delighted to have Merton in this particular issue because so many people of his stature didn't even answer. I remember I had a marvelous letter from Alan Watts after the issue came out. He said he was really sorry that he hadn't answered, because he would have been honored to be in a publication alongside Merton and alongside the other names in there, like Bertrand Russell, Norman Mailer, and Albert Camus.

We selected Merton's poem as the first piece, and I think a few lines from "Chant to Be Used in Procession Around a Site with Furnaces" will show why:

> How we made them sleep and purified them.
> How we perfectly cleaned up the people and worked a big heater.
> I was the commander.
> I made improvements and installed a guaranteed system taking
>   account of human weakness.
> I purified and I remained decent.
> How I commanded.
> I made clean appointments and then I made the travelers sleep,
> And after that, I made soap.
> I was born into a Catholic family,
> But as these people were not going to need a priest,
> I did not become a priest.
> I installed a perfectly good machine.
> It gave satisfaction to many.
> When trains arrived, the soiled passengers received appointments
>   for fun in the bathroom.
> They did not guess it was a very big bathroom for two thousand
>   people.
> It awaited their arrival, and they arrived safely.
> There would be an orchestra of merry widows, not all the time,
>   much art.
> If they arrived at all, they would be given a greeting card to
>   send home:

"Taken care of with good jobs, wishing you would come
  to our joke." . . .
You smile at my career, but you would do as I did if you knew
  yourself and dared.
In my day, we worked hard.
We saw what we did, our self-sacrifice was conscientious
  and complete.
Our work was faultless and detailed.
Do you think yourself better because you burn up friends and
  enemies with long-range missiles without ever seeing what
  you have done?

I don't really know how to classify him as a poet. I would say he
was primarily a religious mystic who couldn't escape the real
world and he wouldn't allow his conscience to escape the real
world. So it must have been a conflict all his life between retreat
and attack.

The only time I met Merton in person was when he came to San
Francisco on the way to the Far East; it was several years after we
published his piece. I knew he was coming. We picked him up at
the airport, and then he stayed at the City Lights editorial department on Filbert Street, in San Francisco—a tiny little two-room
apartment. We went for a walk in the evening and I remember, as
we sat at a table in the front window of Malvina Coffee Shop, he
was quite interested in any beautiful woman who walked by. A
natural Trappist interest—why not? I took him to the airport the
next morning, and that was the last anyone saw of him in America. It was a great shock to hear that he'd died. But I thought that
he had finally resolved the conflict about a Trappist remaining
silent. There was very little to be found out about how he died, so
. . . he just disappeared.

He disappeared into silence.

II. MERTON THE PROPHET

Ernesto Cardenal

We are living in the greatest revolution in history—a huge, spontaneous upheaval of the entire human race; not the revolution planned and carried out by any particular party, race, or nation, but a deep, elemental boiling over of all the inner contradictions that have ever been in man, a revelation of the chaotic forces inside everybody. This is not something we have chosen, nor is it something we are free to avoid.
                                                    —*Conjectures of a Guilty Bystander*

Ernesto Cardenal, fifty-eight, is the Minister of Culture of Nicara-gua and its most celebrated poet. For two years, he was a Trappist monk at Gethsemani and a novice under Thomas Merton, who wrote an introduction to one of Cardenal's books of poems, "Gheth-semani, Ky." After leaving Gethsemani, Cardenal completed his studies and was ordained a priest in 1965. He started the community of Solentiname shortly thereafter. The community became a focal point for the theology of liberation, spiritual renewal, creative arts, and work with Nicaragua's poor. After years of harassment and government threats, it was finally destroyed by forces loyal to Presi-dent Somoza. It is currently being rebuilt under the Sandinista gov-ernment.

I was twenty-three years old and studying at Columbia University in New York when I first came across a book of poems by Thom-as Merton; then I read his book, *The Seven Storey Mountain*. From then on I could not resist. I read all of Merton's books, and also translated his poems into Spanish.

At the age of thirty-one I underwent a radical religious conver-sion and decided to dedicate myself totally to God. And I felt that the best way to be alone with God would be in a Trappist monas-tery. So I wrote to the only Trappist monastery I knew of, which

Translated from the Spanish by Kristina Borjesson.

was Gethsemani, and to Abbot Fox, whom I had known about from Merton's books. He wrote back saying that since I was from a tropical climate, surely I would not be able to stand Gethsemani. So I asked him to recommend a Trappist monastery where I could devote myself to my mission, and instead I received an application form for Gethsemani. I felt this was a sign of God's will for me to go there.

After, I found out from Merton why. The abbot was going to reject me, but Merton felt very strongly that some inner voice, like that of God, was telling him that it was very important for this man, Cardenal, to come to this place.

I felt it was an incredible privilege to be instructed by this great master of mysticism who for so many years had been my master through his books. But when I would meet him for spiritual guidance, he would ask me about Nicaragua, Somoza, the poets of Nicaragua, the Nicaraguan countryside, poets from other parts of Latin America, other dictators. He would tell me about his poet friends, of letters he received from them, about his life in the outside world, about his youth, about Columbia University. And at the end of the session he'd ask me if I had any spiritual problems, and generally I didn't have any so I'd say, "No, I don't have any." And if I did have any, he would resolve them in two or three sentences.

After I left, I'd have the impression that I'd wasted precious time that should have been devoted to spiritual guidance. Gradually, I began to understand that he was giving me spiritual guidance. Because at first I thought I'd have to renounce everything when I entered the Trappist order—my books, my interest in my country, in politics and the dictatorship of Latin America, in Nicaraguan politics, in Somoza, in everything. And, Merton made me see that I didn't have to renounce anything.

He saw no conflict in the contemplative life and a life of action. In the beginning he might have entered with the same attitude as I, but he demonstrated to me that I could still be interested in all these things.

Merton transformed me completely during the two years I was

a novice under him because I thought I was going to be leading a life totally immersed in the spiritual world, giving myself to God and renouncing all interest in literature, politics, and all the things that I had left behind.

As we talked at Gethsemani, Merton said he wanted to establish a community in Nicaragua that would be different from that of the Trappists. At first, Rome was considering giving him permission to do it, but then they withdrew it. About this time I developed a chronic headache, and the doctor at the monastery told me I couldn't continue and had to leave. Merton said it was providential that I had to leave because he wanted to establish the community right away, and that it would be better if I went and got up the necessary support and that he would join me later.

On the day that I was leaving I went to receive his blessing and the last thing he told me was that if he couldn't leave, I was to start the foundation in Nicaragua regardless.

While I was waiting for him to join me, I studied for the priesthood and was ordained in Nicaragua. Then I went to him to get final instructions for the foundation, and he said he still didn't have permission to leave. He was living as a hermit in the monastery, and couldn't help with the founding of the community, but as its spiritual director he said he would visit from time to time.

So I founded Solentinane, and I corresponded very frequently with him. At first, I was alone, and I thought I was making a mess of things, and Merton told me not to worry, because later there would be so many people that I would have a real problem, because I would have to start rejecting people. He was right; after a while there were so many visitors that at times we would have to send them away.

Things were very crazy at the beginning, and I asked him what rules to establish for the foundation of the community. The first rule, he told me, was that there would be no rules. Merton could say this at this time in his life because he didn't have any particular mental bias any more. He wanted to establish a community where there were no habits, no rules, where the faithful could coexist with the communists—and this was before Vatican II.

You see, Merton had entered a religious order that had more rules than any other order in the world. He put up with them— and this he told me—but he didn't agree with them. And sometimes he'd say that monastic life was like living in a circus. It was a circus, because it was a ridiculous life. He said that new ways had to be established. He said that contemplatives today could do as the Desert Fathers did years ago. They were people who didn't only resist the decadent lifestyle in Rome or in the other cities of the Roman Empire, but went instead to the desert and lived separately in solitude. And they hadn't had any religious instruction; they led normal lives in nature, alone with God, for nature is man's natural element, like the fish in water. Also, Merton gave the example of the ancestor, St. Bernard, whom Merton really admired. After being locked up in a cell in a monastery for seventeen years, he was taken out and put to work in the courts mediating disputes between kings. So sometimes the contemplative— because of the situation in his day—must go back to the world and become involved in it.

And so, we at Solentiname found it necessary to participate in our country's political life in the struggle against Somoza, to join in the struggle of the Sandinista Front, after it had been established. And this action was due to the message that Merton had imparted to me, and that I conveyed to my community, which was that we couldn't try to be contemplative unless we also committed our fates to that of the country—to its political life, its social and economic life, everything.

Merton was always our spiritual guide in the community. In 1968 he wrote me a letter telling me he was going to Asia, and that on his return from Asia he would be in Chile at a Trappist community there, and that before returning to the United States, he would come to Solentiname to stay for two or three months. We were making a little straw house for him to stay in when he arrived. We were expecting him at any time when I received a cable from Gethsemani informing me of his death in Bangkok.

Merton's message is still very much alive today. And as far as Nicaragua and Central and Latin America in general are con-

cerned, I can attest that Merton would have supported the Sandinista revolution, he would have supported the liberation of Central America, the liberation of all Latin America. It was God's will
that I went to the solitude of a Trappist monastery, that I left it,
and that I founded Solentiname, where I was for twelve years.
After, I took up the task of the revolution. And right now I'm
involved—my entire culture is involved—in this task. Merton
would support all this, because it is the will of God expressed in
reality.

Much is said about Merton and nonviolence and back in the
days when I was in the monastery, Merton spoke a great deal
about Gandhi to the novices. He made us listen to a record of
Gandhi's. Even so, he told us that Gandhi had said that his method
of nonviolence would not have worked in Hitler's Germany, that
it had only been possible against English imperialism, but not
against German Naziism. And certainly in Somoza's Nicaragua it
would not have been possible to fight using only Gandhi's
method. That is why we act as we do today.

Joan Baez

We have to have a deep, patient compassion for the fears of men and irrational mania of those who hate or condemn us. . . . We have to consider the fact that in its provocative aspect, non-violence may tend to harden the opposition and to confirm people in their righteous blindness.
—Letter of Thomas Merton, quoted in
Merton, A Pictorial Biography by James Forest

Joan Baez is a songwriter, a folksinger, and social activist. She started singing in coffeehouses in 1958 and went on to perform at the Newport Folk Festival, colleges and concerts, Carnegie Hall, and in numerous American and foreign tours. Eight of her albums have sold over one million copies. She went to Hanoi during the Vietnam War, and after the war visited refugee camps. She is a founder of the Institute for the Study of Non-Violence and the human rights group, Humanitas.

I first heard of Thomas Merton in the way names were kicked around in the 1960s when we were looking for cohorts and were just a ragged bunch of outcasts most people thought were nuts. We tend to forget, but some of the first people who began to legitimize the peace movement were priests and nuns. About that time somebody told me about this Trappist monk who was an outspoken antiwar activist—or at least as active as he could be in his confines. So I read some of his poetry and thought, "It'd really be fun to meet this guy."

I don't think I was invited to Gethsemani—I think I probably invited myself. I'm not sure what I read first of his but it must have impressed me, because whenever anybody's willing to speak out, take risks in their convent or their church—whatever it is—it's impressive.

I guess it was in 1967 I went to see Merton in Gethsemani with a friend of mine, Ira Sandperl. We rented a car and drove down from Louisville—by then used to being nervous in the South. We stopped and asked directions in a very redneck-looking gas station, and I think we left before they even gave us the directions because they made us so nervous. Ira had a beard, and I looked like a hippie. Anyhow, we found the monastery and immediately sensed that sort of phony aura where you think, "Oh, I'm going to really see holy people around here." But what we found were monks looking like regular people. And Merton? He was just an absolute doll. All he could think about instantly, which broke my mythical aura in a hurry, was getting out of there and getting a hamburger. And I thought, "Of course, he's stuck in this place and eats gluten bread and grains and nuts and what have you." So we went out to a place nearby and got him two hamburgers, a milkshake, and french fries. And we went out in a big field. He ate all that (we ate half what he did) and started talking. We didn't really know each other yet, so we talked about the movement and Thich Nhat Hanh. I remember him talking about Nhat Hanh; it was clear he adored him. He asked some factual things, about the peace movement and who was doing what, and I guess in a sense we brought in fresh news from the outside. He got certain things in there, but he was eager for firsthand stuff. He knew how isolated Gethsemani was.

After we had our picnic in the field, we came back to his hermitage. He pulled out a bottle of Scotch and began to drink, and we talked for about nineteen hours more. Now we were getting more comfortable, and Ira started pushing him: "Why don't you just go to Bangkok?" Merton said, "Well, that's a good idea but you don't understand this life. You take vows, and one of the vows is you do as you're told to do." But obviously some things about him were not that style at all, or he wouldn't be writing that kind of poetry, and he wouldn't be outspoken against the war in Vietnam. So we teased him about it and pushed and said, "Come on, you seem like the kind of guy with a lot of get-up-and-go. Why don't you just get up and go?" He said, "Oh, no, I can't. . . ."

As we sat there talking to him I could see that he was a strange combination—he was this good, obedient monk, and he was a rebel, a rebel as a Church person. And I imagine that man tucked so far away but speaking so forthrightly gave priests and nuns and other Church people the courage to take steps they wouldn't otherwise have taken.

As for me, I'm very susceptible to spirituality. When I see somebody who I think is spiritual, or who moves me spiritually or even a spiritual setting, I get spiritual. I'm not sure what it was about him—maybe just his basic decency, and the fact that, by his stories and the way he laughed, it was very clear that he was also a human being. And that's very important, because all of us are looking for the guru. And at the same time you know *the* guru has to be a phony. Merton started talking about a party he'd had with some nuns. At the end of a party he said he couldn't resist the extra bottle of champagne. He began drinking it all by himself and he said he watched three nuns who had been watching him all evening, who obviously, sigh, were looking on their hero Thomas Merton. He watched the three nuns turn into nine nuns while he polished off the bottle of champagne. At first I thought, "Oh, gosh, that's not what I expected to hear," and then I thought, "Joanie, you idiot! You know it's very important that you know he is a human being. It's encouraging to the rest of us dummies who have all the same impulses."

Merton shared my feeling—I guess I should say that the other way around—about passive resistance as opposed to nonviolent resistance. They're all very technical terms, but I think it's worth mentioning that Gandhi really tried to change even the wording of *"passive resistance";* he didn't like it because it's so easy to think of nonviolence as something passive, where you don't do anything or where you lie down and let trucks run over you. So he used the word *satyagraha,* which means "truth force." When he tried to put that in English, it came out "nonviolence." I think the key difference is that the traditional pacifist says, "Let my little light shine; I will do my good within my small community in my short life." But *radicalizing* pacifism means taking it into conflict. And I think that's what Merton did when he took a stance, when he wrote the poetry he did and when he made it clear that he had a political position. He preached nonviolent activism, within the limits that he had set around him. Within the structure and the strictness of his life and its Rule, he was an activist. People might question his credibility and say, "Well, he was really safe behind the walls of Gethsemani, to write what he wanted to write and say what he wanted to say." I think at that point each of us has to look at ourselves and see whether we've really confronted our limitations to the extent that we can. In his life he pushed his activism to the outer limits, far more than many of us.

Merton was also remarkably consistent in his nonviolence, and he had many, many followers around the world. Of course, his words are interpreted in various ways in very complicated real-life situations. I came up against this when I visited Ernesto Cardenal in Nicaragua, who says that Merton and Gandhi are his spiritual directors. Now this poses a lot of questions, but in Nicaragua, obviously change for the better had occurred during an armed revolution. For Cardenal, there wasn't enough of a nonviolent movement to do anything, so *he* moved—literally, in one breath—saying he was a Gandhian and Mertonian advocate, and in the second breath saying he was raising money for arms for the revolution. He wrote a long essay on why that's legitimate in a situation like Nicaragua's today. I'm not comfortable with that—at a certain point to say, "Well, at this point I can't follow Gandhi or Merton." To say, "This is my own struggle and I'm solving it this way, I have to raise arms for the Nicaraguan revolution." I don't think Merton tried to work things around for the easiest or surest route. He had enormous integrity, and if you want to follow Merton, then don't claim his name.

For me he was a caring and brave, creative human being whom I knew many, many years ago. And aside from mounds of gorgeous poetry, Thomas Merton left behind a lot of people who loved him. And for me the most outstanding thing, aside from memories of him, happened recently when I was in Sweden and I saw Jim Forest. He gave me a copy of Merton's poem about his brother who died in World War II, and it set off one of those all-night confrontations with myself. I'm not really sure what happened, but I was very moved by the poem and wrote a song, from the poem mostly, finishing up about four o'clock in the morning. I knew his brother had died, and that night it was clear that if he could have given his life for his brother he would. And so, in the song, he gives his life to his brother: "Take my breath, and take my death and buy yourself a better rest . . . beneath the bells of Gethsemani," which was his own home. There was a generosity, a kindness, some sort of overflowing that I felt, and so I wrote "The Bells of Gethsemani."

I think that none of our lives are really worth much unless we're willing to be serious about some things. For instance, my parents taught me when I was little—and for some reason or other it stuck about the sanctity of human life. And I picked that up from them because they were serious about it, and it's become the most important thing in all the things I do.

But most of us tend to take *ourselves* more seriously than anything else. And when we do that, it's an enormous bore—and I think it's that way with most of the phony gurus here in California, which is the guru capital of the world. They're short on humor. But Gandhi was funny. The time I spent with Martin Luther King was laughing. I mean, we just laughed. That's how you survive. And the time that I spent with Thomas Merton, we mostly laughed. It's a very important, life-sustaining activity.

James Forest

At the root of all war is fear; not so much the fear men have of one another as the fear they have of everything. It is not merely that they do not trust one another; they do not even trust themselves. . . . They cannot trust anything, because they have ceased to believe in God.

—*New Seeds of Contemplation*

James Forest, forty-two, was an editor of the Catholic Worker *newspaper and lived in the New York Worker community with Dorothy Day, in the early 1960s. He was a leading figure in the Catholic Peace Movement during the Vietnam War and was jailed many times for his protest activities. Since 1977 he has lived in Holland and is currently the General Secretary of the International Fellowship of Reconciliation. He is the author of* Merton: A Pictorial Biography *(1980), published by Paulist Press, (Ramsey, New Jersey) and* Thomas Merton's Struggle with Peacemaking, *(1984), published by Benoit Press (Erie, Pennsylvania).*

Thomas Merton was the parish priest of the Catholic Peace Movement. There were several people who played important roles in the spiritual leadership of the peace movement, and Dorothy Day was one, certainly. But Merton was someone to whom you could go to confession, who could give you advice about your vocation, who might be able to tell you where you were missing the boat, what you might be doing, and get you back in line again. Throughout those days I often thought, "The Catholic Church is not for me." I would get so annoyed at a bishop's statement or at what our church was failing to do or see, and I would just want to give the whole thing up.

And then, without pausing or condemning, Merton would be able to say, "If you leave I'll still be your friend." But then he'd add, "But you know there is more to it than that. Where are you going to go? What are you going to find?" He could talk about the Catholic peace movement as being one that would touch the Church if it was a movement of love, if it really cared for people, as you would with somebody in your own family whom you truly cared about, but who didn't understand what you were talking about. The Church could change; it would grow into this.

The beginning of my own relationship with Merton started at the *Catholic Worker* in 1961. Dorothy Day was corresponding with Merton. At the time there were many who considered her a kind of heretic simply because she believed that Christians shouldn't kill anybody. She seemed outrageous to the Church in the early 1960s, not to mention before that time. And here was Merton, who was to Catholicism something like Billy Graham to the Protestants, one of the most famous people in the Church, writing marvelous letters to Dorothy. We'd all sit around in a circle, and she'd read the letters—along with letters from anybody else in the country, for that matter. And we'd talk about them, and she'd hand them out and say, "Well, you answer this one, and you answer this one."

One day, she handed me one of Merton's letters and said, "You answer this." I said, "Me? Answer this letter? You've got to be kidding." She said, "Yeah, you're interested in monasticism and you're working on the paper; we're going to publish this. You write in the subheads, and write him about this whole business." So I did. It was "The Root of War Is Fear," which was published in the *Catholic Worker* in October 1961, and which later appeared in *New Seeds of Contemplation,* except for an opening paragraph he had written especially for us. It was a beautiful piece, still one of his best peace essays. This was the first article he wrote for publication in the *Catholic Worker.* Out of this first contact with him grew a correspondence and a friendship, which continued until his death.

Soon after this first article he invited me down to the abbey. So I hitchhiked down with Bob Kaye, a friend from the *Catholic Worker.* It was in the middle of winter, it took three days, and we got there absolutely exhausted. I immediately went to the chapel to pray. I was a pious Catholic, down on the knees whenever possible. Bob was a much more practical Catholic, and he collapsed on his bed in the guesthouse. I'd been in the chapel just a few minutes when I heard this muffled but enormous burst of laughter. I couldn't believe it. A Trappist monastery in my imagination did not include laughter. Here, people are supposed to be fasting to death all the time; praying on their calloused knees; this is serious stuff.

But it became impossible to pray with this continuous laughter, so I got up, went through the various fire doors that led back to the guesthouse and stood outside Bob's door for a minute—as this turned out to be the source of the noise—wondering what was going on. These gales of laughter were still coming out of his room. And I thought, "Well, Bob has had a nervous breakdown. It's understandable. Three days of hitchhiking under such circumstances, from the Lower East Side in New York to some remote part of Kentucky, needless to say, he's finally flipped out." I opened the door, and indeed Bob was laughing and so was this monk on the floor who was in his black and white robes, big leather belt around him, feet up in the air, clutching his belly, his face as red as a tomato. I didn't for a moment know what they could possibly be laughing about like this; I had never seen such laughter in my life.

My first gasp gave it away. Bob had taken off his shoes! After our three days of hitchhiking, the room smelled like New York's Fulton Fish Market in August. It was an incredible aroma. And I suppose to Merton this was the *Catholic Worker* as a house of hospitality incarnate. The smelly Catholicism that we were practicing on the Lower East Side had arrived in this clean place, this scrubbed environment. And he just laughed and laughed and laughed.

Merton could be the most lighthearted and umpremeditated joker, like a mad, crazy truck driver. And then, suddenly, he could switch to the most intense, sublime, antibaroque theological stuff, beautiful to listen to. I recall this Polish friend of mine, an agnostic, down at the abbey, sitting on the porch of the hermitage and blurting out, "I do not understand the Mass! I have never been able to accept that, that there could be some kind of divine intervention. I can't believe it. What about it? Explain the Mass to me!"

Merton immediately started talking about the Mass as a kind of dance where in fact time does break into eternity, and eternity breaks into time. That there was this sudden connection of grace in our lives. If we are willing to imagine it could happen, it happens. It was just beautiful. I wish I could say exactly what he said that day. It was wonderful the way in which, in an unthreatening, unprotective, totally undefensive way, he explained what he thought the Mass was all about. The word *dance* I remember particularly—"This is a dance, we are doing a dance, and God is in this dance. And that's what we're doing at the altar with all these ritual gestures, the dance."

I can remember walking with him and talking to him about vocation, and again this deep seriousness came over him. Nothing jovial. This was life and death stuff, like the convicted criminal who can save his life if he succeeds in walking across a crowded marketplace carrying a cup of water filled to the brim. If he doesn't spill a drop, he is saved. But if he spills a single drop, the executioner walking behind him cuts his head off at the same moment. That kind of solemnity and stillness would descend on him, and it took my breath away.

People often see these tranquil pictures of hooded monks at Gethsemani and imagine that the monk's life, and therefore Merton's life, was just one blissful, contemplative day after another. Well, it wasn't at all one big happy community at the abbey. It was just like any big family, and Merton had his share of hostility. I remember walking out of the great building with Merton, through a subterranean concrete passageway, and down at a bend in the passageway was one of the monks, reading the *Catholic Worker*. He had it at arm's distance, glaring at the page. He looked up from the *Catholic Worker,* saw Merton and me, crumpled the paper up and threw it into a garbage pail that happened to be there. And then he stormed off. This was the first year of Merton's involvement with the *Catholic Worker* in a public way, and things got worse later on. Merton's response was immediate laughter. Then he told me this same monk had criticized him in his early years as a writer for not being concerned enough with events outside the monastery, and now he was furious that Merton was too concerned with news from beyond Gethsemani. "I just can't get it right!"

You see, Merton was causing all kinds of waves with his writing. His first essay for the *Catholic Worker* said, in effect, "The way Christian ethics are going now, before you know it people will decide it's OK to kill your next door neighbor if he tries to get into your private fallout shelter. We're getting so privatistic, and self-absorbed, and indifferent to others that this is the logical extension of it all. You don't need to wait for the Russians—you start killing your next-door neighbor." Well, this essay appeared in the *Catholic Worker* the very same week that an article on the same track, but in the opposite direction, was published by another theologian who actually said that under certain circumstances you may have to kill your neighbor if he's trying to get into your fallout shelter. "After all, there are only so many cans of soup, and you're going to have to be down there a certain number of days before it's safe to come out." Merton was amazed. His own imagery was meant to shock, and now he himself was shocked that Catholic theologians were already coming up with a moral code, an ethics for the fallout shelter, in which the most immediate enemy was the neighbor. "Pretty soon," he said, "we'll decide that under certain circumstances it would be OK for St. Peter to kill St. Paul."

At the end of 1965, despite the internal controversy in his abbey about his peace involvement, we at the Fellowship of Reconciliation (FOR) arranged for a retreat of peacemakers with Merton at Gethsemani. A. J. Muste, who had long been the secretary of the FOR, went down; and Tom Cornell, managing editor of the *Catholic Worker;* Dan and Phil Berrigan; W. H. Ferry; John Howard Yoder, the Mennonite biblical scholar; Tony Walsh from the Catholic Worker house in Montreal; and several other people. We had a week together. Shortly before we left for Gethsemani, I recall

Merton sent out a sheet of questions that he wanted us to think about. The first question is the only one that I clearly remember now: "By what right do we protest?" I thought, imperiously, "That's a very strange question, you know. What do you mean, 'By what right do we protest?' " Indeed! "By what right do we breathe?" But more and more I've come to appreciate what a very important question this is. What gives *us* the right to make a noise, to bother people with our particular concerns and worries? At our retreat this question forced us to look at the deepest source of protest. Is this something that really comes from heaven? There's no other right to do it. There's no other right to annoy people and disturb people as peacemaking does do. It is as easy to make things worse, despite good intentions, and to drive opponents into greater rage and violence, while imagining you're a great hero, an instant saint.

I think the main thing Merton did on that retreat was to keep bringing things back to basic questions, over and over again, and not letting them drift off. You can so easily go off on a tangent with righteous indignation. In the midst of his playfulness, that kitten quality of his, he had this astounding discipline and concentration, a clearness and detachment, an aim like Robin Hood's, and this was very important for us.

During that week he wouldn't let things wander very far. He would let our ranting go for a way and then he would say, "But!" He was constantly having these "buts"—"Yes, but let's not make that the whole thing." This was very helpful in those days, which were both heady and desperate. It seemed as if nothing that we did made any impact on the government. They were still burning people to death in Vietnam; in fact, burning more each day. Nothing we did, nothing we said, no price we were willing to pay seemed to matter. It had no braking effect whatsoever.

We wanted to do something more "serious." And Merton would say, "It *does* matter what you're doing. If you stick to the truth and the decency of the thing, it matters. It may not have immediate, visible effect but it isn't wasted. And if you get swallowed up in desperation, you'll fall into all kinds of traps and go up all kinds of dead-end streets, and then it really will not matter; it will feed into violence, it will not have the effect you think it will." So it was a kind of extraordinary patience, really a Benedictine patience, that he was constantly bringing to us. And the value of doing something just because it was truthful.

He had other recommendations, some that probably still strike people as far-fetched. Merton was very enthusiastic, for example, about a walk from San Francisco to Moscow—a peace pilgrimage, really. He thought one of the things American people had to do was to make contact with their unmet enemy. Jesus says, "Love your enemy," yet so many of us never even think of visiting our enemy or even consider reading our enemy's books or seeing his movies. Not too many of us had read Dostoyevsky or Gorki or Tolstoy. If we're going to read a book, we're probably going to read some popular potboiler.

He felt we were not willing enough to do the things that connect us. And so, when he visualized a little peace movement project walking across America, and then finally arriving at Red Square, he thought that was a very good idea. Anything whereby you connect yourself with that person you have the least respect for, the least contact with, if it's a bum on the Bowery or a commissar in the Kremlin. And for a peace movement especially it had to make these kinds of bridges: Get to know the Cubans. Don't just read what the President says about them. Find out about them yourself.

At the same time, he was aware that people active in peace work were often better at loving people far away than up close. In their fury with the continuous murder going on in Indochina, many people were trashing the government. They would look at the White House and imagine the man who lived there as someone simply to hate. "This guy is no good, this guy doesn't care, this guy is just busy burning people—he enjoys burning people—that's his hobby." Merton thought these people in government were trapped, and the peace movement had to help them out of it. If we condemn them and rage at them, they're just going to burn more people, that's all. If we don't see the connection between us and them, how easily we could have gone the same way ourselves, then they're going to become less and less able to see it as we see it. ✎

There were two distinct sides to Merton, equally intense, equally needed by a man with such breadth, such energy. Oh, he would sit there with the most avid attention to everything that was said. Ping Ferry once said about Merton, "He was like a kid going to the circus." He said this describing Merton during those final days before leaving for Asia, but you could say this about Merton much of the time throughout his life. As far as I could tell, Merton was permanently interested. He had the curiosity of a kitten; there was nothing in the house that wasn't worth exploring. There was nobody not worth talking to; he listened to everybody with wide-eyed attention, often scribbling down notes.

Occasionally you'll see a photograph of him walking. I can remember Merton, between meetings at our retreat, just going off into the woods near his hermitage and walking back and forth, back and forth. Sometimes he had his notes. Sometimes he had nothing. Sometimes he had a rosary. He prayed a lot in those spaces, and he was thinking; that was clear.

Yet when we came back together, it wasn't all talk. We had beer, we had candy bars . . . but then we'd get into these very intense discussions about the war in Vietnam and where we were going and what, as peacemakers, we could be doing. That retreat was one of the most powerful weeks of my life.

He was a man of such tremendous energy, such a prodigious output of books, and yet at Gethsemani he was somewhat of a mystery. I remember one of the monks at the abbey, the guest-master, Brother Francis, saying to me, "How does he write those books? Where does he find the time?" Of course, I had less an answer than he had. But I happened to come out of the novitiate one day, where I'd sat in with the novices for his lecture. Merton was still master of novices at the time and he decided to grab this little moment to write a letter. And he sat down at this big office Royal, a really shlocky typewriter, and started banging away. It sounded like a machine gun. I wouldn't have been surprised if the typewriter had burst into flames as he kept going at it for five more minutes, flailing away at those keys. I'd never seen typing like that before.

As it happened, he was writing a letter in defense of the monastic life to somebody who had written saying, "What are you doing there, in this time, with so much crisis going on outside your walls? Why are you a monk?" And he came up with this great essay. He said, "The only place you can stop the war in Vietnam is to be where you belong, where God wants you to be. If you're in the wrong place, there's nothing you can do. If I give up where God wants me to be, I can do nothing. It's just a question of being where I'm supposed to be. Not where I want to be." In fact, he frequently thought about leaving, going here, going there, but constantly came back to his realization: "This is where God wants me to be."

Not that it was easy to be there, or easy to be a writer. As you discover in his journals, there were times when he wanted to shut up completely and do nothing, just be in direct contact with heaven, period. No typewriters, no letters. No visitors. No nothing. This was one of his recurrent big ideas. And then the next day he would be thinking about going to Moscow as a peace hostage, to live on the target of U.S. missiles. There was a space when he very much wanted to live in a Moscow apartment so he could say, "Don't drop a bomb; there are some Americans here, too." He thought seriously of doing that. Then there was a time when he was all set to go to Mexico and live at Christ of the Resurrection Monastery. Later on he was drawn to Nicaragua and considered living at Solentiname with Ernesto Cardenal. In the last year of his life, he thought about Alaska and was all set to live in a hermitage up there. Then, in Asia, he looked for a place to live in the Himalayas. At least once he considered coming to the Catholic Worker community to help serve soup. He had lots of plans, lots.

None of these plans was realized, and yet each enriched his monastic life. By imaginatively throwing himself into all those far places and different cultures, everything he did as a monk was continually being enriched. He didn't go, physically. He didn't set up his hermitage in the foothills of the Himalayas. He didn't serve soup at the Catholic Worker, but all these yearnings of his became part of his life as a monk and writer.

It's interesting to look back on Merton's upbringing, to try to see how he developed. Merton was in England in the 1920s, just at the time when Gandhi was being discovered by the English people —not as an enemy of the Empire but as a different sort of opponent, something totally new to them. The kind of resistance Gandhi developed was something they had never before experienced. Merton was fascinated by all this and wrote a paper on Gandhi at that time, at his boarding school, Oakham. This was not appreciated, incidentally, by most of the people with whom he was studying.

He became a Catholic just as World War II was getting started. It was already well under way in the part of the world he knew best, Europe. So he was more aware of it than were many other Americans. And he made the remarkable choice *not* to be a soldier. For a Catholic at that time this was unheard of—Catholics were still struggling for acceptance and tended to be more patriotic than the Presidents. But in becoming a Catholic Merton had to ask questions that perhaps most Catholics born to the faith would never think to ask. For him it was all new stuff. It was very much based on trying to figure out what this Jesus was all about. The question was "What would Jesus do?" And he could not imagine Jesus killing anybody. It was for that reason, as he says in *The Seven Storey Mountain,* that he became a conscientious objector. His brother volunteered to fight in the war and died in it, and Merton respected that choice. He had a great deal of respect for those who didn't see it his way.

Then Merton left The World—at the time this was the way it was put—and he went to The Monastery, truly with a capital *M*. This was supposed to be very holy and contemplative. But he gradually discovered that you can't walk out on the world. You may be called by God to the monastery, but no one is called by God out of the world. There's a remarkable passage in his journal book, *Conjectures of a Guilty Bystander,* in which Merton describes a pivotal moment in his life that occurred in the late 1950s, ten or twelve years after the publication of the autobiography that had made him world famous. As I recall this, he was assisting a Trappist visitor who only spoke French, which Merton spoke fluently. He had taken the man into the nearby city of Louisville. He wasn't wearing Trappist robes but was dressed as an ordinary priest—black suit, a Roman collar. At the time no photo of Merton had been published so there was no possibility of anyone recognizing him—in fact many of his readers probably imagined a very skeletal sort of person who had barely survived all that Trappist fasting and midnight prayer and hard, physical labor. At some point Merton was on his own. He stood at a certain streetcorner, looking around, and it was as if the shingles suddenly fell from his eyes. He realized his oneness with all these people. The fact that he was a monk in those remarkable medieval robes out there in the enclosure of his abbey while all these people were wearing their Woolworth's stuff here in the city—all this didn't make any difference. God is just as intimately and caringly involved in the life of the least person on the street, someone who may not have been in church in twenty years, as with any monk or bishop. He had this overwhelming sense of connection, which was really one of his main "enlightenment experiences." It was a turning point in his life and the direction he afterward went as a monk. He was no longer up there on Mount Everest rubbing elbows with God while the rest of us were living blindfolded on the plains below. Among other things, the huge correspondences he got involved with date from after this quiet but explosive moment on that streetcorner in Louisville. His correspondence with Dorothy Day and the *Catholic Worker* dates from this time, and his connection not only with peace people but Zen teachers and rabbis and many, many others.

His involvement with Dorothy Day and the Catholic Worker movement was an important part of his last ten years. In Dorothy, Merton recognized a woman who at first might seem to be living the most noncontemplative of lives but who was actually another contemplative whose "monastery" was a house of hospitality that found Christ by welcoming those who are lonely, who suffer, who are abandoned. Merton saw the connection with his own vocation. It wasn't just that the world was being saved by the Abbey of Gethsemani, it was being saved wherever people were being faithful. Dorothy Day became for him a real representative of faithfulness. She was a woman of the poor. She was saved because she recognized Christ in the poor. And she was saving the world and the church by sharing that vision. For Merton this often meant reconnecting himself with nonviolence, in the active sense of Gandhi or Martin Luther King. The Gandhian influence in the Catholic Worker—peace work, going to jail, protesting the works of war and destruction—this reanimated a part of himself long neglected.

So it's not hard to see why he was in his later years often walking a tightrope, trying to write things in a way that would be acceptable to the censors, yet saying rather radical stuff that he felt had to be said. This was extremely difficult and yet occasionally he spoke to friends of it having a positive side. "Well, the censors are generally extremely nationalistic and militaristic—but these are exactly the same kind of people I'm writing for, ultimately. So by trying to get through to these censors, perhaps I'll do better at reaching others too." And so he would see some challenge in this. But other times he would be exasperated that the censors were really not interested in the truth at all. They just wanted to present to the world this homogenized product called "Thomas Merton," to make him look good, to make him look as nice and clean as a piece of packaged cheese manufactured in the dairy of the Abbey of Gethsemani. He was furious about that.

We would get these telegrams at *The Catholic Worker*—"NO FINAL APPROVAL RECEIVED YET, BUT EXPECT NO MAJOR REVISION." We were trying to meet the deadline for the next issue, but still the censors hadn't come through and we wanted to have the big Merton article all laid out. And then, thank God, at the last moment, we would receive the message: "ARTICLE FULLY APPROVED, GO AHEAD." So we'd get it in, and then he would write a letter a few days later giving us the blow-by-blow: "Well, we had to go all the way to the abbot general in

Rome, who was wandering around Europe at the time, but we did get it through."

In the 1950s, before I knew him, when in fact I was in high school and had no idea he existed, I understand from Naomi Burton Stone that he had been silenced for a time. Apparently his superiors thought his spiritual life needed a period of nonwriting. But in the 1960s he was silenced because he was disturbing conservative Catholics by insisting that peacemaking is a religious obligation and should become a normal part of Christian life. Peacemaking, he said, is not an option like stamp collecting or joining the choir. This was not something that a lot of people wanted to hear at the time. There was anger. He was actually accused of being a communist or being used by the communists. The *Catholic Worker* was said to be a communist publication, and so he was writing for this communist publication. He wrote me that the abbot general in Rome had heard from somebody in the FBI that Merton was being used by the communists. So, finally, he was silenced. He had just finished a book, *Peace in the Post-Christian Era,* and they said, "Sorry, that can't be published." And it never was.

But honestly, I think to him it was a relief, in a way. In fact he wasn't happy with some of the things he was writing. He was trying to write not just what was crucial to himself personally, his conviction that Christ doesn't kill people, that Christ is not in the killing business . . . when you get right down to it, Merton was a basic Franciscan, someone who wouldn't touch weapons . . . but he was trying to write for people who subscribed to the familiar "just war" theology. This was what the Church was generally accepting, and he had been trying as much as possible just to own that and then to say that he wasn't entirely pleased with it, that it didn't work in this world of missiles and germ warfare and nuclear bombs. Merton was trying to understand rather than bury opponents with his superior mind and skills as a writer. So when the silencing came, he began to write under other names. And that was great, that was very freeing for him: No censors. No big name for people to worry about. Nobody cared what "Benedict

Monk" wrote for the *Catholic Worker*. He could write about nudism if he wanted to, anything at all, the monastery didn't cae. But in fact he wrote about the arms race and peacemaking. As long as Thomas Merton's name wasn't on it. One letter was signed "Marco J. Frisbee!"

Over the years, as I've thought back on Merton, his life, his legacy, the very rationale behind his life, it's come clearer and clearer that he was a man of remarkable fearlessness about life . . . and yet so aware of his own limitations and needs. I think he helped many of us to become less afraid. He used to say, "The root of war is fear." He helped us see that the root of our parochialism is unvarnished fear. Our fear of ecumenism in those days was fear. We were afraid of Protestants, we were afraid of Buddhists, we were afraid of Jews, we were afraid of just about everybody. But Merton wasn't. As people got to know him better and his books became more and more clear on all these enthusiasms— Zen masters, Desert Fathers, Jewish Hasids—he let us know we didn't have to be defensive, that we could be open to these things. And in the years since then we've seen the Church growing constantly in these directions. Merton helped it happen. I expect he celebrates the news of it daily in heaven.

But he knew his limitations well, and I think that was one of the main reasons Merton actually went to the monastery and stuck with it to the end. You know, he was wildly enthusiastic about women. He just thought they were terrific, the best thing God ever did. And he liked looking at them and being with them. He enjoyed their company. And I think it was extraordinarily hard for him to withstand the temptations he had to become another male Don Juan. So he went into the monastery partly because he knew he needed a special communal situation in which to live. Also he liked to drink. He thought that beer and whiskey were a very good idea. I have a poet friend, Ron Seitz, who went out into a meadow one day with Merton to read poetry and talk, and they brought out two or three six-packs. Ron downed perhaps one or two beers, and Merton drank the rest. Joan Baez remembers getting drunk with Merton. Merton had difficulties, we would say, with these things. And so he put himself in a kind of environment that had built-in special spaces, as well as certain brakes and limitations that helped him overcome his more self-destructive aspects and to channel his energies. It wasn't easy for him, nor was it easy for others on whom he depended, especially his abbot. At times he was really miserable with the limitations and seemed to complain bitterly about them with God, his friends, and himself. But there are certain outstanding results that have come from his being there. I can't help but thank God he kept at it.

III. MERTON THE FRIEND

Robert Lax

To name Robert Lax in another way, he was a kind of combination of Hamlet and Elias. A potential prophet, but without rage. A king, but a Jew, too. A mind full of tremendous and subtle intuitions, and every day he found less and less to say about them.   —*The Seven Storey Mountain*

Robert Lax probably knew Thomas Merton longer and with greater consistency than anyone else. They met at Columbia University shortly after Merton came to America from Cambridge University in England in 1934, and their friendship continued through the rest of Merton's life. They wrote each other extensively, and some of those letters have been collected in A Catch of Anti-Letters *(1979). Lax, a poet, now lives in a simple house on a remote Greek island —a life not dissimilar to Merton's, who at the end of his life lived as a hermit.*

Describe what Columbia was like in those days and meeting Merton.

What I was most interested in was working on the college humor magazine, or on the college literary magazine and taking courses with people like Mark Van Doren and Jacques Barzun and Lionel Trilling. So I went as fast as I could up to the *Jester* office where Ad Reinhardt was the editor. I'd first heard about him (Merton) because he wrote a couple of funny pieces in *Jester*—and they were really professional. And I said I'd like to meet Merton. Herb Jacobson, who by that time was the editor said "he wants to meet you, too." We went to the big dining room in John Jay, not the grill where we usually ate. Merton was already at the table, and Jacobson took me over and introduced me. Merton looked up and shook hands, and it was really an amazing meeting right away. It was the friendliest look, the friendliest handshake I'd ever remembered. You know, there was no question in my mind that we were friends from that moment on. And Jacobson left us, and we talked about a lot of things—mostly about *Jester,* I guess, but I've read people later who talked about meeting Merton, and apparently it's always that same experience.

He already was wearing some sort of—I don't know why, maybe because he'd come from England—but he was wearing some sort of a business suit, or a three-button jacket. And his hair was brushed more than ours was likely to be, and he looked as though he'd already perhaps worked downtown or something. There was nothing lost looking about him.

What about those days up in Olean?

The first year there was [Ed] Rice, Merton, and I. And I think all of us had been writing for a long time, probably through grammar school and high school, and later in college, and now getting out of college. We thought we'd get up there and write our novels. It wasn't a new idea, like something we found in a magazine. Merton had written his first novel when he was eight years old, but he'd never found a place as good as the cottage in Olean to sit down and write one then. When he found it, he sat down and wrote a real novel. Saroyan was writing at that time, and I think he had written a novel in a week, so that sort of inspired us. We didn't do that, but we were going at it pretty fast for that reason.

What were you fellows thinking about; what did you want to accomplish?

We really had to take our own lives and our own work seriously. We wanted to be making some sense within the social pattern. And there were plenty of people who were examples to us, to keep us at that. Even if we weren't into the Young Communists League or something like that, we were challenged by it. And there were people like Meyer Shapiro, who was teaching art history, and Mark Van Doren, who would keep us remembering the world. Merton had a good paragraph (in *The Seven Storey Mountain)* in which he talks about his father—saying that art is not something that is just to excite the emotions or anything like that, it really is a form of contemplation. Already he knew that, and if we went up to Olean to work it was because we felt we could do something that was going in the opposite direction from the whole commercial world. We'd already had our brushes with that world, and we didn't like it. We didn't like the standards that we'd have to conform to in order to move ahead in that world. That's why we were going up to the woods.

There was a section in The Seven Storey Mountain *where Merton said that the only worthwhile pursuit in life was to be a saint.*

Merton was already in the Church by that time, and he was wondering what he wanted to be; he didn't seem to have found an identity. He didn't want to be a professor or a novelist and he was already making progress in his spiritual search and I must have asked him what he wanted to be, and he said he wanted to be a good Catholic. At that point I said, "No, what you want to say is that you want to be a saint. If you want to be a good Catholic, you want to be a saint." And he said, oh, no, he couldn't be that. And I didn't believe he was right there, I thought that if you want to be a saint, God will help you, it's what he wants you to be too. And so all you have to do is want to, actually to want to, and you'll have the help you need. And that seemed like a surprising idea to him at the moment. He told Mark Van Doren about it, he said that I was running around saying that all you had to do to be a saint was to want to. And Van Doren said, "That's right." So, then he had to give it some serious thought.

Could you try to trace the steps of his conversion and the appeal of Catholicism?

I think a lot of things were happening that none of us were aware of and that he wasn't aware of. I think he was moving toward Catholicism because it was time to move toward Catholicism, toward his way of life. Right after my graduation from college we both went up to Olean, and at some point on that trip I said that I had been interested in Neo-Thomism, and the things that Richard McKeon and Mortimer Adler were doing out in Chicago, and Thomistic thought in general. This was in June 1938.

Merton said that if there was one thing that he wasn't much interested in, in the whole world of philosophy and religion, it was that tradition. That he really wasn't interested in Catholicism at that point, that he had been interested in Chinese thought, Chinese philosophy. That summer when he went back, he started reading Gilson and also Gerard Manley Hopkins, and suddenly a lot of Catholic books were just falling into his hands, and by that November he was being baptized at Corpus Christi Church.

What was it in Catholicism that drew him?

I think the feeling of God's concern for the world, God's mercy toward sinners, actually made a strong appeal. I think that it never occurred to him that that was at the center of Christianity. But it seems to me, he certainly was supernaturally moved toward all this because he'd be sitting in his room reading, and suddenly he hears a voice inside him saying "Go to Mass," and soon after that he hears a voice saying "Go and become a Catholic," or "Go and talk to Father Ford about becoming a Catholic." And he wasn't given to hearing voices. I don't know how to describe what voice he heard, but it was certainly a strong impulse to do this. He just couldn't resist it, he couldn't say no.

When he eventually made the decision to go to Gethsemani, what was your reaction to that?

I think by that time I was just very pleased. I hoped it would be right, and I believed it would. He certainly had been looking for a vocation. He was writing pages of journal about this search for a vocation, and when he went out to visit Gethsemani and came back—I think I was working at the *New Yorker* at the time—you could see that it had made a tremendous impression on him, and that he had found something he really liked. I didn't know then that he'd actually go out and join, but I thought he'd be visiting there often.

What was Merton like when you visited him for the first time at Gethsemani?

It was Christmas time and the first time that I saw him was at

Mass, but the next day I had an appointment to meet him and the abbot at the same time. I was waiting to be let in, and as I stood in the hall I saw a monk who was sitting on the window ledge either reading or in prayer. And he looked very medieval; the whole monastery was looking very medieval to me, and he really seemed to sum it up. And at some point someone came out of the abbot's office and told me that I could come in, and as I did the monk came to life too, and it was Merton. He was wearing his robes all right, but he was as funny as ever and completely recognizable. It was really the old Merton. But at that moment in the window frame he wasn't, he was just a medieval monk.

His ordination day?

In the pictures of Merton's ordination day, you'll see that he looks much younger than he did in his college pictures, or in anything leading up to that. Rice took some close shots, and he does look as though he had been reborn and very young. I remember when we were still in Olean he was beginning to look, well, like a successful, but middle-aged, novelist. At this point he looked like a novice. He had a really young face, and he was also very happy at this time.

What was Thomas Merton seeking?

I think he was just looking for a direction in life. I think if a tree is looking for a direction in life, it's just hoping to become a tree. And I think that what Merton was hoping to become was completely a human being, or completely Thomas Merton. I think that that really was what was moving him all the time, and any decisions he made really were leading toward that, and he hoped that they would lead him toward that. I think that he felt blocked at one point or another in the choices that were offered him, say, by the university or by the world or anything else, and that if he was drawn to the monastery, it was because he could see a kind of freedom there—paradoxical—but a kind of freedom in which he could grow and become fully the thing that he must have felt he was potentially. And so what he was after was to become himself.

What were the swings in mood that he would have in the years at Geth-semani?

I've never been very good at trying to psychoanalyze my friends. I usually watch what they're looking like physically and let it go at that. And when he seemed low to me, it was as if his health wasn't going well. That first year it looked as though he was having trouble, I don't know whether it was with his lungs, but he was certainly in weak condition. Probably from trying to adjust to a new sleeping schedule, a new diet, and whatever other pressures may have been on him. And he did have trouble with his health on and off through his stay at the monastery.

But in his books, he always talks about interior struggles.

Funny, I think I've found out more about his interior struggles and his whole interior life when I read his books than I ever did in talking to him. When we talked, neither of us talked very much about our interior lives. If we were talking about them, I think we were talking about them obliquely. We would talk about world problems and they may have had their relevance to our interior lives, but I can't remember his ever talking to me very much about an interior struggle.

What did he make of his success?

I think he was happy about it because once he was in the monastery, whatever success he had was for the greater glory of God. I think that he was fulfilling his vocation in that way, and he was glad to see it happen. And I think he really turned himself inside out in these books because he felt that was his vocation too. I think that he knew he was fulfilling this role, and he wanted to make it quite clear that this is what happens when a man is alive and struggling and conscious of it and articulate about it. And that was because he was going through it not just for himself, but for many people. When he suffered a thing, if he suffered anything, he felt that he should explain it first of all to himself, and explain it in clear-enough terms so that anyone else who wanted to know what was going on with him or with a human being in general, could

find out in regular and traditional terms. He wasn't talking his
own language to himself, he was talking the language of the West
or the language of the East and the West to himself.

When I was traveling, I'd meet theological students and people
like that who had just encountered his books for the first time, and
they'd always say, "He was talking as though he was talking from
inside of me." He was so much inside himself that he was inside of
everyone. And they always felt a very personal bond with him for
that reason, because they'd been looking for a bond I guess with
themselves, and then here they found an articulate bond with
themselves in another person.

Tell us about his turn back toward the world.

When he first got to the monastery he might have thought that
he could live just a contemplative life out off from the rest of the
world. That may have been an illusion that he had when he first
got there, like the euphoria anyone could expect would soon wear
off. I think he sounded least like himself in paragraphs where he
was saying that sort of thing. At least to me, it didn't seem like the
whole Merton. It seemed like a part of him, a part that I could
expect to change again. When he got back to a more universal
point of view on philosophy, whether it was Sufism or Buddhism
or accepting any of the great traditions in philosophy in and out of
religion, that was the Merton we already knew before he got in
there and it was just parts of him coming back.

I think he certainly had a strong social conscience when I first
knew him at Columbia and when anyone knew him at Columbia.
He was certainly interested in the problems of the whole world.
And even at his most solitary and contemplative period of his early
entry into Gethsemani, I'm sure he was still conscious of the problems of the world, but as he settled in all these things came back
and he realized that he could deal with them from within the monastery.

I think that all the things that were happening at the end of the
1950s and through the 1960s in America certainly got to him because he was in touch with key people in all the movements and he

couldn't have been himself, he couldn't have been corresponding with them without responding in a very alive way, and a responsible way. He knew, I think, he couldn't say, "Don't get into action, just live a contemplative life in a limited sense." I think he realized that contemplation and action go together, and he could see a way of combining the two.

He was writing about Gandhi, and he said that this is Gandhi's lesson and his legacy to the world:

The evils we suffer cannot be eliminated by a violent attack in which one sector of humanity flies at another in destructive fury. Our evils are common and the solution of them can only be common. We are not ready to undertake this common task because we are not ourselves. Consequently, the first duty of every man is to return to his own right mind in order that society itself may be sane.*

And I think that's where the relation of the contemplative life and the active come together.

Those last days before the Asian trip? What was going on in his mind and his life?

There's no doubt that he was ready for a trip, and that he was ready for a long one, and that Asia was the right direction. Certainly he'd been moving in his thought and in his studies in that direction. And it must have been a very welcome invitation to go off to Asia and talk to people who were in a monastic tradition. By that time he was much more attached to the idea of monastic life, the contemplative life, a hermit's life, than he was to the specifics of any particular sect or religion. I think that he found that the monks of all religions were moving in the same direction and whether he agreed with Teilhard or not in all things, he certainly agreed with him in the idea that all things that go up must converge, and he could feel that particularly those in all the monastic traditions of the world were beginning to converge and to a point where you could go and talk to a whole circle of contemplatives and all in the same language in a sense. So he was ready for it in

---

* Introduction to Mohandas Karamchand Gandhi, *Gandhi on Non-Violence,* edited by Thomas Merton, (New York: New Directions, 1965), p. 16.

that way. And his trip out to the West just before that, out to Redwoods, had also been very exhilarating for him. It gave him the idea that he might be able to stay within the monastic framework as a monk of Gethsemani and still live as a hermit out there in California or in some other place.

This following quote is from a journal Merton kept six months before he left for Asia. And I think it gives a picture of the movement of his thought at that point. He says,

In our monasticism we have been content to find our way to a kind of peace, a simple, undisturbed, thoughtful life. And this is certainly good, but is it good enough? I for one realize that now I need more. Not simply to be quiet, somewhat productive, to pray, to read, to cultivate leisure. There is a need of effort, deepening change and transformation. Not that I must undertake a special project of self-transformation. Or that I must work on myself. In that regard, it would be better to forget it. Just go for walks, live in peace, let change come quietly and invisibly on the inside. But I do have a past to break with. An accumulation of inertia, waste, wrong, foolishness, rot, junk. A great need of clarification, of mindfulness, or rather, of no-mind. A return to genuine practice, right effort. Need to push on to the great doubt. Need for the spirit. Hang on to the clear light.*

Finally, his death

I was in Kalymnos when I heard about his death in Bangkok; my sister phoned me. I think she'd gotten a letter from Abbot Flavian Burns, and she must have told me, in very gentle stages, about it. And, after she told me, she asked me if I thought I was going to be all right. I told her, yes, I thought I was going to be all right. I hadn't understood it well, though. I thought that he had found a live wire somewhere in the street just by accident. I hadn't really gotten the details. Anyway, I was quite rocked by the news. But what I did was go into a church there, a small church I'd often gone into, and prayed.

---

* *Woods, Shore, Desert: A Notebook, May 1968* (Albuquerque: University of New Mexico Press, 1983), p. 48.

Did you feel you'd lost a . . . ?

I can't say that, I really can't say that, because I really . . . and I don't feel it now. In specific ways, I certainly felt I'd lost a correspondent; if I had something funny I wanted to tell him about it would be a little more difficult now, but I didn't feel lost. I didn't feel a maudlin thing about it at all. I felt that he'd gone on to another stage, and I really felt that if it happened, it must have been the time for it. I think probably most of his friends felt that way. I'm sure the monks pretty much did. But it's one thing to feel that, it's another thing to actually experience the loss over the years—the feeling that you really can't drop a letter to him. Eventually you do feel back in touch, I think, anyway.

Georges Linières

Here, in this amazing, ancient town (St. Antonin) the very pattern of the place, of the houses and streets and of nature itself, the circling hills, the cliffs and trees, all focus my attention upon the one, important central fact of the church and what it contained. Here, everywhere I went, I was forced, by the disposition of everything around me, to be always at least virtually conscious of the church.
                                                        —*The Seven Storey Mountain*

Georges Linières, age seventy-two, was born in St. Antonin, France, where he was a schoolmate of Thomas Merton. After a career as an elementary school teacher, M. Linières is now retired and lives in nearby Montricoux.

Thomas Merton came to Saint Antonin in 1924 with his father when he was about nine and, though I was a little older than he, I was friendly with him because he was very lively, very nice, and because he had a certain manner that made it easy for a person to be interested in him. I think he admired me because I was older, and because I was known as a sportsman. My friends and I found him somewhat peculiar because he wasn't dressed as we were at that time. So to us he was a stranger; we called him "the English boy," even though he was an American. I still remember he was wearing pants that we'd never seen before, knickerbockers. He was also wearing some strange shoes. They were what we wear now, baskets. We were about seven or eight years behind America in those days; now, thanks to the media, we're not so far behind. But then, whatever came out in America came much later to France, and even later to the provinces. But he was nice, he was eager to learn, very friendly and a little mischievous, too—he liked to play jokes. And when I played jokes on him, he didn't take it badly.

Translated from the French by Kristina Borjesson.

When the movies came to St. Antonin, they were shown in an abandoned Protestant temple, and Mr. Merton played the piano there. He had a big pipe, I still remember that, and while he was playing during the movies, often you could see smoke rising from the pipe. He played jazz—which was strange music to us, we'd never heard it before. And his accent was a bit strange to us too, but we found him to be very nice, like his son. I think the people of St. Antonin took to him like they took to Thomas. He didn't have a mother then, so he lived with his father in—shall we say?—a bohemian fashion. Sometimes he was somewhat haphazardly dressed, with one leg of his pants hanging down and the other torn—but he was totally oblivious to it, he didn't give it a second thought.

Thomas was considered to be a little prodigy at St. Antonin because in one or two years he learned what it took others three or four years to learn. He was, according to his instructor, my friend M. Gagnot, the best student he ever had in French. He got the best grades. So you see, his vocation as a writer had begun back then.

Those of us who knew him in those days were very surprised by his conversion. I think perhaps he was a Protestant but he didn't go to church. As far as the Catholic Church goes, I know he didn't go to the Catholic Church. I don't think there were any signs of his future vocation, not at all. He was neither a dreamer nor did he have any complexes—he was very freewheeling, honest, and lively.

I mentioned that he was pretty mischievous, so my friends and I didn't hesitate to play a joke on him one day. He came to the square where the Church of St. Antonin was located, near the pastry shop, with two letters in his hand.

We asked him, "Where are you going, Tom?"

"I'm going to the post office to buy some *timbres* (stamps)" When he heard the word *timbres,* my friend shook his head, and looked at me with a perplexed expression on his face.

And Tom, of course, began to worry a bit—that he'd mispronounced a word or hadn't understood us.

My friend said, "What does *timbres* mean?"

"*Timbres* are what you put here at the corner of a letter," Tom said.

And my friend said, "Oh, those aren't *timbres*. Here in St. Antonin we call those"—and he said the first thing that came into his head—"*troboules.*"

Tom looked at me for assurance, and I assured him my friend was right. So Tom went confidently off to the post office, while we walked behind him and hid behind a window to see what would happen.

He walked up to the clerk at the post office and he said, "Madame, I'd like some *trouboules.*"

The clerk, who knew him well, said, "*Troboules*—what does that mean, is that English?"

And Tom said, "No, ma'am, it is St. Antonese."

And the clerk said, "*Troboules,* I don't know that term."

"It's to be put here, ma'am," Tom said, and pointed to the corner of the letter.

And the clerk said, "Oh, you mean *timbres.*"

And, of course, we were behind the window, laughing.

John Barber

His greatest sermon was on the thirteenth chapter of First Corinthians, but
his exegesis was a bit strange. . . . There he stood, in the plain pulpit and
raised his chin above the heads of all the rows of boys in black coats and said,
"One might go through this chapter of St. Paul and simply substitute the
word *gentleman* for *charity* wherever it occurs. "If I talk with the tongues of
men and angels, and be not a gentleman . . . a gentleman is patient, is
kind." "
—*The Seven Storey Mountain,*

*John Barber, age sixty-nine, graduated with Thomas Merton from
Oakham School, Rutland, England, in 1933. After taking a degree
from Cambridge University in 1936, he returned to Oakham in
1945 to be a teacher and schoolmaster, and he now lives in retire-
ment in the town.*

Old "Merty," as we called him, and I were at Oakham at the same
time, that is, the late 1920s and early 1930s. We were both in the
sixth form, and when we left Oakham we both went up to Cambridge together. You can't really judge what Oakham is like today, compared with the time Merton and I were here, because
there is so much that has changed. It was a small school in those
days; there were only up to two hundred or so students. And it
was not a big or famous school as it is now. It was not very highly
intellectual, either, and I would say by and large that Merton was
too well geared for a school like that. But he was a friendly type,
a bit headstrong, but never arrogant. We all mucked in together,
and he made a lot of good friends because he had the kind of
intellect you could respect and not resent—he was never the type
to vaunt his superior mind.

I suppose you might say that he had a moody side, but I
wouldn't say it was moody as much as it was a way of withdraw-
ing into his own thoughts. He thought deeply, you could sense
that, much more deeply than most of us who came from a less

international background. He read philosophy, he read religion, he read a great deal over and beyond anything he was expected to know in school. And I would say, even with his bright, sprightly nature, he had a contemplative side. He appreciated being on his own a good bit. That was the strange contrast in him.

I can't see that he picked up much religion at Oakham. The religion at the school in those days was what you might describe as "muscular" Christianity. There wasn't much real theology in it or depth of thinking. It was, I would say, rather shallow, and in that everybody had to go to services whether they wanted to or not, it was to some extent perfunctory. And there was a rough element around, a certain crudeness that Merton wrote about in *The Seven Storey Mountain*. I think that sprang largely from the fact that the culture of the average lad wasn't all that deep. Many of them came here for, say three years, and left without very much qualification. They could read and write, spell, and were fully equipped to go into business or work, with their fathers or the farm, but that was about it. Not a great percentage of them went to university, so we were on a lower gear than he was, by and large.

The English public schools in those days were a bit snobby, and the thing to be was to be a gentleman and have all the values of a country gentleman. This was a legacy from the nineteenth century, I suppose. But it was very much in the forefront, and the chaplain used to bring it into his sermons, equating gentlemanliness with Christianity, making them interchangeable. I think Merton found this rather shallow—assuming that if you behaved yourself and acted properly everything was OK. Merton, who had seen more of the world than most of us, saw through this. He wasn't the type to point the finger and say, "That's a sham," but he saw through some of our English ways. There may have been limitations on our academic and cultural horizons but as far as friendship was concerned that was all on the level. We got on very well with him because he was such a great chap to involve himself in all that was going on.

If I had to visualize Tom Merton today, in his Oakham schooldays, coming across the lawns on the commons, he probably wouldn't be walking. He'd bounce or run across, bubbling over with enthusiasm. And he'd probably have some hare-brained scheme for what he was going to do next. It probably wouldn't have to do with work, it would be about the next game of rugger or a party he was planning or something like that. There was no middle ground for him. Yes, he did things to excess, whether they were good or whether they were bad. And of course it was excesses that brought about his Damascus Road experience. He just threw himself into everything. He wasn't naturally a gamesman, he was a slightly clumsy bloke in some ways, but he threw himself into it when he was at school because it was the thing to do.

He had very great coordination in his brain box but not in his limbs. For instance, in cricket he was no good at all. But rugger is a game that, if you set yourself to it and muck in hard, most people can make a shot of it—and he did just that. He played very hard among the forwards, and I don't remember whether he got his color cap, but he stuck in and nobody felt he was letting us down; everyone appreciated his guts.

He did good things to excess and got credit for them but he was inclined to go off the rails and do bad things as well, which eventually got him into trouble when we went up to Cambridge. He was a wildcat at Cambridge and he used to go drinking and off with girls, probably not the right kind of girls very often. We used to go on the Cam River and mess around in punts, though we weren't very good at it. I remember on one occasion we were having a bit of a party in Ray Dickens's room, and suddenly Merton comes up the stairs, dripping like a drowned rat. He had fallen in the river, so he walked straight through the party into Ray's bedroom and set about changing his clothes. One hell of a racket was going on, so the owner of the shop came up and stepped into the room. And just as he was about to shout at us for making such a noise, he saw the partly open door of the bedroom and an expanse of naked flesh, which of course was Merton changing. He drew the wrong conclusions, and he yelled out, "Get that naked woman out of my house!"

I think most of us at Oakham and Cambridge were very surprised that he should have become a Trappist monk. On the other hand, we realized that he had the intellectual ability to do whatever he took up, to perfection almost, and he did just that. He had the innate capability of that type of dedicated life. But, even then, from all I hear, he was a bit of a wildcat as a Trappist. They kept him on the reins at times, and they made a lot of concessions to him, did they not? I believe they'd have to, to hold him where they wanted him and not to lose him by being too strict—and that just about sums him up. He was always, at school, kicking over the traces. But, by and large, he believed in doing what he wanted to do, and he also believed in not getting caught.

W. H. Ferry

If I have broken this silence, and if I have been to blame for talking so much
about this emptiness that it came to be filled with people, who am I to praise
the silence any more? . . . Have men of our age acquired a Midas touch of
their own, so that as soon as they succeed, everything they touch becomes
crowded with people?   —*The Sign of Jonas*

*Wilbur H. "Ping" Ferry was a founder of the Center for the Study
of Democratic Institutions in Santa Barbara, California, and one of
the center's fellows when he began a correspondence with Thomas
Merton in 1961. They sent each other thousands of documents and
letters by mail (Letters to Tom, a private printing, was published
in 1983), and Ping was a frequent visitor at Gethsemani, especially
once Merton had moved to the hermitage. Today, Ferry and his
wife, Carol, live outside New York and work with peace and justice
programs.*

The picture of Tom Merton that many people have is one of a
monk who wrote marvelously affecting, marvelously instructive
books of solemn and profound religious importance. I didn't see
very much of that. I saw the other side. I saw a concerned citizen.
A beer-drinking good fellow out taking pictures of barns and cem-
eteries and roots and things like that. A man who liked to walk in
the woods and talk. A man who was furious with the way the
world was going and couldn't wait to tell people of his fury.

Ours was a friendship I never wholly understood. I didn't have
much to offer him and didn't have his intellectual hardware. I
suppose it was our mutual concern about the state of the world
that was at the bottom of it. But our times together were never
heavy or burdensome. Tom was merry and very good company;
his language was lively, abrupt. He saw the world with first of all
charity, second wisdom, and third of all with a marvelous sort of

irony. You could see it in his writing: after carrying on for a long while about, let us say, the then Catholic view of the development of weapons, he would say, "I'm getting strident; I'm beginning to sound just like the opposition."

I first went to see Tom about four or five months after he wrote to the Center for the Study of Democratic Institutions saying he liked what we had produced and that he'd like to participate in some way. He was a legend even in 1961 because of his books and because of the essays that were appearing, largely in the Catholic press, but sometimes outside. And so I was absolutely delighted to have this opportunity to go into a strange country called Gethsemani and meet this fabled man, even though I didn't know how he could "participate."

I don't remember everything about our first meeting but I do remember that he said, "Come to the back gate and bring some beer and a couple of sandwiches, and we'll go off someplace and take some pictures and sit and talk." Beer was an indispensable ingredient of our meetings at Gethsemani and I soon learned that the way to the back gate was the proper way to meet Tom and that the six-pack of beer was expected.

He was just beginning to write on secular issues and he said he was delighted to see me, to meet the source of so many remarkable documents the center had sent to him. Merton was the country's principal document gobbler. He read everything and anything and as I'm a considerable document pusher myself, we had a good relationship from the start. He subscribed to *Le Monde* and to a British paper, but no American papers. His Number One souce of intelligence during the years that I knew him, as far as domestic situations were concerned, was Izzy Stone. *I. F. Stone's Weekly* he characterized in several letters to me as his lifeline.

His was as capacious a mind as I've ever encountered. He took everything in, fitted it together, and somehow it came out always in an orderly way. It was a good thing that he chose the essay as his way of dealing with the world. He was a monk and he just had little hunks of time to write. But in two or three hours it's amazing the cogent gems he could turn out. He was an exceptionally sensitive man, as well as an exceptionally religious man. The race situation, the bomb—he saw the consequences clearly and early, and from a place so far out of the mainstream. He was years ahead of almost everybody in his concern that the machines were going to take over—the whole business of dehumanization. And he was quite right.

And now, twenty years later, we are seeing developments that were pretty clear to him in the 1960s. The developments in higher technology, the robotization of factories as well as the fact that the machines are taking over the whole society. Computers have become an intrinsic part of the schools; now they are making their way into the homes. Merton saw a complete change from a society based on humane values to one based on the ideal of efficiency.

Okay, so all this stuff is bubbling around in the mind of a cloistered Trappist monk who is supposed to live a very circumscribed life. You might imagine that he would have his problems. Once I asked him about his vows and he smiled and said, "Ping, poverty, that's a cinch. Chastity, well, that takes a little getting used to, but that's manageable. Obedience, that's the bugger."

His most serious problems with that "bugger" started at the time the first forays were being made into Vietnam. He was appalled by the kind of conversation that was going on in Catholic circles over the "just war" theory and the possible use of the H-bomb. He started telling the world about his indignation. And then the trouble began.

He never knew where the pressure came from; not from Abbot Dom James alone, it came from someplace above. His understanding of it—although he had a very analytical mind, he never investigated it very carefully himself—was that it started with ecclesiastical higher-ups in Washington. He was aware that a lot had been stirred up by some of the things he had been writing about: war and peace and pacifism and the duties of Christians. But when his abbot said "stop," he did. "I'm not going to go any further," he said. "It will not do any good, it will just cause a commotion that won't be good for anybody concerned, including the church."

This was a prudential judgment. He wasn't backing off, he just knew this too would pass, as it did pass, and all of the materials he was so concerned about getting out during the 1960s did appear, and were just as worthy when they came out later.

But, believe me, there was a lot of impatience and a lot of huffing and puffing on his part about this; he didn't like it one bit. Not because he was looking for fame but because he felt people should be aware of what was going on.

When the curtain came down on Tom's literary efforts, when he couldn't publish officially, it made quite a change in my life. He asked me, and I suppose others, in effect to be a bootlegger for him. The prohibition, the rule that he could not publish, ran only against magazine articles, books, and such things. He was allowed to send around mimeographed copies. And at that point in his life he was producing essays, sometimes at the rate of one a day. It was the understanding that I would take these mimeographed copies and distribute them. He furnished me with lists, and I had a good many lists of my own. He warned me against allowing his essays to be printed without permission, but he didn't warn me very hard. I had a red-hot Xerox machine at my disposal and people to stuff these things in envelopes and put names on those envelopes and shove them in the mail. Well, this heightened our relationship a great deal.

There were our mutual social concerns, there was this special relationship that we had once he was censored. And then there was the incident in 1966 that made me see that he was not only a religious, moral figure but a man, simply unadorned, a man. It was at that time when he was under a lot of attack from within the Church, outside the Church, and even from members of his own order. He was having his usual stomach problems, and on top of that his back was giving him terrible pain. I think it was one of the lowest points in his life. He was fifty years old, and he was vulnerable.

Tom called me, and very rarely did he do that. He asked me to come as soon as I could to the monastery—he had something to talk to me about. And he said, "Bring a lot of change—bring a pocketful of change." I couldn't imagine what this was all about.

He walked around to the back gate where I was waiting dutifully with a couple of hamburgers and a six-pack, and he said abruptly, "I've got to make some phone calls. Let's go." He told me in the car that he wanted to call a woman he had met recently. "I'm just terribly taken by her."

Well, I was flabbergasted by this. I said, "What's all this money for?"

"I gotta make a phone call."

"Well, you don't need $5 in change," which I had in my pocket.

"Maybe I will. We've gotta get a long way away from the monastery. I can't be seen making a phone call any place around the monastery."

We went about twelve miles away, and we stopped at a gas station that had one of those phone kiosks outside and nearby a picnic table, where we put down the beer. Tom rushed over and then came back. The line was busy. And over the next two or three hours he rushed back and forth to that phone just like any man exasperated because he couldn't get hold of his girl. But this was Tom Merton, and I thought it was quite funny. He saw the humorous part of it, too, but he said, "It isn't funny, I've got to talk to you about this, but I've got to get this call through first." Well, it took quite a long while, quite a few hours, quite a few busy signals, and he finally gave up.

We went off and sat and talked. There's one very serious proposal that he made that cannot be regarded very seriously today, but he said, "What I want to do is go away with this woman for a month. Just for a month. What do you think of that?"

I said, "Tom, are you out of your mind?"

"Well," he said, "what's wrong with it?"

"What do your superiors have to say about this?"

"I don't think I'd consult them very much. I could do this. There wouldn't be any publicity about it."

"There wouldn't be any publicity? You'd just disappear from the monastery, and this woman would just disappear from wherever she comes from, and the world would pay no attention to this?"

"You think there'd be any publicity?"

"I'm sure there would. I'm absolutely sure."

"Well," he said, "that isn't what I wanted to hear. Do you suppose there's any way of handling it?"

And I said, "On this I'm going to fail you because if there were a way of handling it, I wouldn't help you. I think this is a mistake. I'm not being moral about it, I think it's just a big mistake."

We talked about it a lot more and he said, "You've given me something to think about." We went back, and before we got to the monastery he said, "Look, here are two telephone numbers. Will you try to get through for me and pass a message?" And I said, "I'm afraid I can't even do that. I don't mind being mixed up in something I believe in, but I really don't believe in this very much."

Before I left the next day, we had about two hours together. The only thing he said was "Thanks for the conversation. I got hold of her this morning. Thank you." I never knew how it all came out, or how he settled with himself. All I know is that this woman, whoever she was, was a remarkably sensitive, terribly nice person. She managed her side of this very well. I'm sure she did nothing to bring this on, so to speak. I saw Tom many times after that, and we spent a lot of time together out on the Coast before his last trip, but the matter was never mentioned again.

When I saw Tom in 1968 just as he was about to leave for Asia, it was obvious he had reconciled things and was generally in much better spirits. He was like a child on his first trip to Disneyland when I met him in Santa Barbara where he stayed for two or three days. He was at last on the last leg of the great adventure. He was full, just full of a sort of quiet joy. He smiled a great deal, laughed a great deal.

So we headed north, up the Coast to look for a spot for a possible hermitage for him; he had an idea that if he would live away from Gethsemani for a time he'd like a place high above the Pacific Ocean. He even had a general idea where it might be; near those nuns at the Redwoods monastery. It's in a remote part of California and the coast is rough. We looked along the Big Sur, we went up into the mountains at one point at Santa Lucia, a mile or two, to see what that looked like, and it wasn't quite right. We went on and on and finally got to Redwoods monastery. Next day I drove him across twenty miles of the worst road in northern California to get out to the coast. There was an open spot where the road ended. We got out of the car and walked over to the bluff and there was the great Pacific in front of us. Tom Merton was grinning from ear to ear. We walked another twenty yards and looked down from the bluff—to see condominiums and a golf course, and restaurants being constructed right down below us.

Oh, that look on his face. . . . He couldn't believe what he was seeing. "Ah," he said, "let's go back. This isn't the place." And that was about all.

There is so much talk about Tom's wanting to get away from Gethsemani, that he was plain sick of it. But I don't think that Tom ever outgrew Gethsemani. He said to me what he said to others: "I'm always going to be monk of Gethsemani." Perhaps if he had lived, he would have spent time in other hermitages, but he knew his true home.

Some weeks later—I'd been in Mexico on vacation with my wife—I called my office to see what had been happening. I hadn't spoken to anyone there for ten days. My secretary got on the phone and said, "The only important thing that's happened is that Tom Merton is dead. He died in Bangkok. The monastery would like to talk to you." I had the phone number, I called up, and sure enough, that was it. I don't remember much after that.

You can believe most deaths, but I couldn't believe that this man, right at the point when he was reaching the summit of his aspiration, which was to find himself, as he would say, "find myself in God," in the circumstances that he had so devoutly hoped for, for so many years. . . . Bang, that was the end of it. It was quite a long while before anybody really accepted that this was just an accident. Which I now do, but I didn't for some time. His death left a hole in the lives of many people—never to be filled. There have been a few great men in my life—three or four, maybe—and he was one of them.

Mary Luke Tobin

The contemplative life is unfortunately too often thought of in terms purely of "enclosure," and monks are conceived of as hothouse plants, nursed along in a carefully protected and spiritually overheated life of prayer. But let us remember that the contemplative life is first of all *life*, and life implies openness, growth, development. To restrict the contemplative monk to one set of narrow horizons and esoteric concerns would be in fact to condemn him to spiritual and intellectual sterility.   —*Conjectures of a Guilty Bystander*

Mary Luke Tobin, age seventy-six, was accepted into the Sisters of Loretto in 1927 at the age of nineteen and in 1932 made her perpetual vows. She was the only U.S. woman who served as an official auditor at the Vatican Council II, and was president of her order from 1958 to 1970. She is the author of Hope Is an Open Door *(Abingdon, 1981). Long active in the peace and justice movement, she founded the Thomas Merton Center in Denver, which functions as a meeting ground for those who attempt, as did Merton, to live both a life of contemplative prayer and of action.*

In 1959, I was living just twelve miles from Gethsemani at Loretto, Kentucky, in the mother house of our order, when Thomas Merton drove over one day with his friend Dan Walsh. Dan had been his Columbia professor, and Merton wanted to find a place for him to teach and give some lectures in philosophy. We were the ideal place for that; we had a little junior college and were happy to accommodate Dan. It was quite a visit, and I remember receiving a letter from Merton a day or so later, apologizing for having caused such a disturbance in our convent. All the white-veiled novices had been leaning over the balconies in an effort to catch a glimpse of this great man. That meeting, and that straightforward response to as much clamor as a convent could muster in those days, was just the start of a friendship that lasted over the next nine years.

Merton was delightfully simple, very human and very affable when you were with him. And I've never seen him with anyone whom he didn't immediately put at ease. He had a very genuine way of relating to people, a delight with every human person. Often we would sit on the dam over at Monk's Pond at Gethsemani and talk about what was going on in the Church, what was going on in religious life, what was going on in the world. It came through over and over again that he was a man firmly committed to religious life as one way to greater freedom for a Christian. But this made him critical of hampering restrictions, and there were plenty of them around in those days.

And while it was a wonderful experience to ask him questions about those times and to hear his own reflections, I never felt in the least bit that "Here's this great person whose presence I'm in." He was just a good, warm, and terribly insightful friend. As I grew to know him better over the years, I realized that Merton was very conscious of his own humanity; he was humble and sincere in talking about it. He was a man who examined himself continually. He blamed himself for being too sensitive to the opinions of others, and he often talked about that as his "allergy." I think he lived with this, as all of us must, but in a person of his depth and sensitivity it must have been particularly painful.

When Merton finally moved to the hermitage, it was an innovation, and the monastery didn't exactly know where this whole idea was going, But I think they valued this very unusual son of the monastery, and so they went along with it. They didn't exactly want the whole world rushing up to his front door, so it wasn't easy for him to show it to me at first. But he wanted to, and the first thing he did was give me a number of colored pictures of the hermitage. Finally, in 1967, he was able to take me there and to show me around the monastery grounds. I'll never forget that day. We went back to the hermitage, and Merton pulled out a set of bongo drums and started beating on them. He was a great jazz buff, and finally he had a record player and some records after decades of silence. He was so happy in those, his last days. He absolutely loved the hermitage; it suited him. The main room was lined with books on shelves up to the ceiling. And on that first day he took me there he looked at his books and said "I am an intellectual really. I spend my morning writing, answering letters. Then, in the afternoon, I go to the woods." I believe what he wanted to indicate was that the life of the mind and the life of prayer were well integrated for him. And he had found the ideal place to experience both.

His writings and his letters indicate what a wide range of interests and concerns he had, but, aside from our conversations about what was happening in the church our talks seemed most often to turn to two subjects: race and peace.

Merton was extremely interested in the whole civil rights movement and what blacks were doing in the late 1950s and early 1960s. Although the word *blacks* wasn't used then, Merton would have immediately used it, and he did at the very end of his life. I think he came to a special consciousness about blacks specifically at the time the Birmingham children were killed. It seemed such an outrage to him; you could see it in his eyes when he talked about racial injustice. He suffered keenly because he identified so closely with those oppressed people. Oppression was not some abstract word to him; he hurt as they were hurting.

Merton gave me a tape with an experimental meditation he did one night in his hermitage. In the background was Jimmy Smith, the black musician, playing on the electronic organ, and there was Merton saying, "I'm sitting here in the woods, the moon is shining, and all the wheels are turning and Jimmy's playing." And you could hear Jimmy's fingers running up and down and Merton, as we used to use the expression, "grooving," singing to Jimmy, dialoguing with Jimmy: "You're right, man, I'm with your people, man, I know what you're saying, I'm against the white backlash, man, and I think anybody who understands what you're saying here, understands the future." It was a marvelous sort of way of saying, "We're all one people, this injustice has got to go, I'm with you."

Eldridge Cleaver speaks of Merton in his book, *Soul on Ice,* and said something to the effect that "Merton elbowed his way into my room and whenever my spine needed to be stiffened all I had to do was read his passage in *The Seven Storey Mountain* on Harlem and I was immediately reencouraged and the flame lit up once again." Merton had had that touch with Harlem in the late 1930s, so he understood what was going on. He predicted the riots at Watts and a whole era of racial violence. When he was doing his Jimmy Smith meditation, it was actually at a time when riots were going on in Louisville. You see, Merton was a great voice in civil rights, and in fact he had been in correspondence with Martin Luther King, and King was coming to Gethsemani for a visit. But then, about two weeks before that visit was to take place, King was assassinated and it was a great blow. Merton felt terrible about that because he felt so keenly that Martin Luther King was absolutely right, coming at it from a Christian nonviolent position. Merton was so in tune with that; he would have loved the visit with King.

Unlike other religious leaders of the era, Merton was always against the split, the dichotomy between spiritual and material, the political and the religious. One of the greatest things I think in Merton's later life was that he was able to tell people that we should overcome that split. He saw reality as a whole, and he felt that it should not be divided up into compartments. For example, in his essay on the nuclear threat, he spelled this out in detail. He explained how compartmentalizing is at the root of our faulty world vision. He even pondered over the actions of some people in the peace movement, wondering if their tactics could be effective. He certainly supported those people, but he questioned the effectiveness of their actions.

What's most amazing to me, as I have said often all these years, is that Merton saw things so far ahead of time. He always maintained that counter-force and deterrence were the most dangerous possible means to use in the Atomic Age, because they could provoke a pre-emptive first strike on the part of the enemy. He was writing things twenty-two years ago that we think we just heard yesterday. And so, it's very understandable, in the early 1960s, to see why Merton was censored. The Catholic community in the United States was, I would say, somewhat disappointed that the great hero, Thomas Merton, was talking about these social issues. They wanted him to talk about prayer and contemplation only, and only in their sense of it. Because the Catholic community in the United States was far from able even to cope with the morality of the Vietnam War, not to speak of the nuclear threat. A simplistic anticommunism was rife in those days, even more so than now. I remember him saying to me one day, when the monastery curbed his writing, "Imagine, I can't write on peace." He looked incredulous and somewhat downcast. I knew it was a time of intense suffering for him.

I appreciate having had the pleasure of knowing him, the delight of having him come into a room, smiling, welcoming, filled with interest about everything in the world, looking for my response. Who could help but love this man? He never was a "guru" to me, but rather a good friend with whom I could exchange ideas, and I value that greatly. He gave people many things through his friendship in person, through his books, but for me it is all summed up in his statement that he saw contemplation not as some abstract, otherworldly act but as reality, the way a person lives: The real within the real. Some of his last words are words that help me guide my own life: "We don't need so much to talk about God but to allow people to feel how God lives within us, that's our work."*

---

*Merton, A Pictorial Biography (Ramsey, NJ: Paulist Press, 1980), p. 99.

IV. MERTON THE MONK

Flavian Burns

Every moment and every event of every man's life on earth plants something in his soul. For just as the wind carries thousands of winged seeds so each moment brings with it germs of spiritual vitality that come to rest imperceptibly in the minds and wills of men. Most of these unnumbered seeds perish and are lost, because men are not prepared to receive them: for such seeds as these cannot spring up anywhere except in the good soil of freedom, spontaneity and love. —*New Seeds of Contemplation*

Flavian Burns entered the Abbey of Our Lady of Gethsemani in Trappist Kentucky in 1951, at the age of nineteen. He was elected abbot in 1968 and was the person responsible for allowing Thomas Merton to go on his Asian journey. After five years as abbot, he did not stand for reelection, instead choosing to live as a hermit on the Gethsemani grounds. In 1980, he was asked to serve as interim abbot at Holy Cross, the Trappist monastery in Berryville, Virginia. He agreed to do so, providing he would be permitted to return to Gethsemani and a hermit's life after his term was completed. Of the forty men who trained with Abbot Burns at Gethsemani, fifteen are Trappists today.

My first meeting with Thomas Merton was in *The Seven Storey Mountain,* and while I was quite taken with the life, I really wasn't that interested in Merton himself. So when I went to Gethsemani it certainly wasn't to see Merton or anything like that, it was for the life.

I really didn't recognize Merton for the first few months because there was strict silence and the priests were separate from the novices. My first realization that this particular man was Thomas Merton of *The Seven Storey Mountain* was almost a shock because he was completely out of character from what I had expected. I had already sized up a few people I thought were Merton but I was happy at the Merton I discovered. I really didn't get to know him personally until about two and a half years later when I entered the scholasticate.

There were about forty scholastics, a very bright and alert group, very open to what he had to say and, in my opinion, sort of sitting on the edge of their seats listening to everything he said, laughing at every humorous remark he made. As for me, I had gone into this life with the idea of dedicating my life to God alone, of living for God alone and of being a disciple of Jesus Christ, period. I didn't believe in being a disciple of just a plain human being. I was a pretty serious young man at the time.

And so I remember sitting in those classes with my hand pressed on the desk saying to myself, "I will not be like them. I will not be a disciple of this man."

But I liked him enormously in the scholasticate—everyone did —because, while he could be serious in his spiritual direction talks, he was full of humor and jokes, and always buoyant.

Like the first time I recognized him in the monastery; it was after the bell had rung and all two hundred monks were filing through the cloisters to the church. And there, coming down the middle of the cloister in the opposite direction, was this one man, making signs to everybody, explaining why he was going in the wrong direction. And then he would tease us in class about not believing in silence. He would say, "Why, you fellows can't even pass one another in the corridor without making some silly sign," which of course he did himself. He was a master at visual commentary, like during the readings in the refectory or during the chapter talks. Just with the raise of his eyebrows or a facial expression of horror at what was being said or proposed, he could bring down the house in laughter.

You see, Gethsemani was a lively place, and it was crowded, which shocked me when I entered. I presumed after reading *The Seven Storey Mountain* to find twenty or thirty old men walking around prayerfully with their hoods up. Actually, the bulk of the people there were teenagers, including myself. It was an austere life, but Dom James, the abbot, had the genius to know that if you are going to live this kind of life you'd better keep your sense of humor and keep things in proportion.

We rose at two in the morning and spent long hours in the choir. There was no central heating, and we wore heavy clothing; that was the hardest thing for me at first. After I received the habit, I felt all the weight of those woolen garments and I thought to myself, after the first day, I will never be able to spend the rest of my life weighted down by this clothing. And I suppose it was hard for most people to come in and have no chance to speak. The food was not that plentiful, but work was. Eating two pieces of bread and a cup of not quite coffee in the morning and then going down and splitting logs in the winter weather, that was pretty rough.

But I think it was a good life for Merton, and I think he thrived on it. He was a nervous energy-type person, but the life disciplined him. When you saw him, even in private, he wouldn't usually sit at a desk, he'd be in constant motion, fiddling with a pen or something. But at meditation in the church, where I was able to sit somewhere behind him and observe him, I noticed that he was capable of sitting for the whole half-hour without moving a muscle or doing anything. I think this is why he was into the disciplines of yoga and other meditation disciplines, because he needed them. His temperament was lively, hectic, and nervous. But he compensated for it by discipline.

Why did he end up a Trappist? At Gethsemani? I don't know, but if you believe in God's providence, it was meant to be. I think his own reasons for going there were probably more like mine, expecting to find a quiet place where he could concentrate on meditation and contemplation. But the life wasn't actually built for that; it was much more active. However, once he made the commitment and saw the inner meaning of the disciplines there, I think he really perceived that "this is necessary for me if I want to get what I came here looking for."

For sure he wasn't the most practical person. He never learned to drive a car, for example. And I think with the electrocution everybody was shocked that this famous man could die in such a manner. The kind of light talk around that sad time at the monastery was "We're not surprised, just surprised that he didn't do it sooner, living by himself in the hermitage." You see, he was quite clumsy at day-to-day things. Otherwise he was actually a very ordinary person. There was no sense of him being famous. Many entered the monastery with that notion after *The Seven Storey Mountain,* but it was very difficult to sustain any kind of pretense, living such a structured, close life.

Even when he very badly wanted more solitude and the privacy of the hermitage, there was never any of: "Hey, wait, look, I write all these books, I do this, I need this something special." It didn't enter into his thinking or his personality. He just felt that God was calling him in that direction, and he was supposed to do what God wants in a monastery.

The only time I ever heard him talk about himself as a famous person was when we were young scholastics and they had a psychological test going around where you wrote down three answers to the question "Who are you?" Merton made us do this, and we gave all these various answers. And he commented on our answers, asking which were the good ones and which the bad ones, and why. The basic thing is, most people answer *what* they are, rather than *who* they are. So one of the young monks asked him kind of challengingly, "Well, what did *you* answer?" And he said, "I was Father Louis, master of the scholastics; I was Thomas Merton, famous author; I was . . . " And he got a big laugh from the group at that, because that's not how we knew him.

Perhaps one of the most misunderstood aspects of his life was his relationship with Dom James Fox, his abbot for most of his years at Gethsemani. Dom James was the fatherly type who considered Father Louis as sort of a boy he had to care for. Merton was already famous by the time Dom James got on the scene because it was the previous abbot who had encouraged him to write and publish *The Seven Storey Mountain.* So here he had this man who was an image of holiness and Trappist life to the outside world, and yet he knew him as the jovial boy who could get into trouble very easily and felt it was his responsibility to keep him in line.

Father Louis came from a bohemian kind of life, and Dom James was Boston Irish, Harvard, an All-American kind of fellow, and there were those built-in conflicts, I think. But, what a lot of people forget, and what is more interesting to me, is that when Father Louis published *The Ascent to Truth*—a rather heavy book on St. John of the Cross's spirituality—we had that read in the refectory. I think it made a great impression on Dom James, who was not at all in favor of monks writing, and Dom James took Father Louis for his father confessor and spiritual advisor for the next fifteen years, even though he was still the abbot who was keeping him pretty close to home.

Father Louis felt confined, that he was being cared for a little too much, I'm sure. But when I took over as abbot in 1968 there were some interesting exchanges, because he knew the relationship would be different. The many requests he had, to speak here, or to go there and do this—which Dom James always turned down—I told him would be his province. And he actually had no great desire to go to all of those things. I remember him coming to me with a letter he had from someone asking him to come and speak in their monastery or convent, and he said, "Can't you just tell them that I can't go?" Yes, he wanted the abbot to tell them that he couldn't go because he didn't want to offend them by telling them that he didn't want to go. I said, "No, we've got the new regime now. Before, you were complaining about that." I simply felt it more proper to our personal relationship, that he take responsibility for these decisions himself.

So a lot of Merton's isolation came from Dom James's desire to keep up this image that Merton had created, through his books, of the Trappist life, and not to go out and dissipate it. It's something like—what do they say?—"Familiarity breeds contempt." So there was a sort of mystique created by the fact you couldn't get to see this person. And I think Dom James thought that was a good thing for the order and for Merton's books and for everything, and that if he got to be known and everybody knew that he was the nice casual guy he was, and not this mystic, the image would be shattered.

When he finally did make his Asian journey, there were good reasons for him, after twenty-seven years in the monastery, to make this trip. We decided that he would take three to six months to see some of the Asian religions, the Zen Buddhists and the Dalai Lama and his followers in reality, in person, because he knew these people only through books and he felt, as he told me, that this was the perfect time to go to Asia, because Asia was getting more and more westernized. And there was a danger that the spirituality they had, the spiritual treasure, might not survive the next ten or fifteen years. We must not forget that this man was uniquely qualified to experience these things and that he would, just by the nature of his being a writer, communicate it to others. I was well aware of his power and his impact, and I was hoping that after his return from Asia he would go into a deeper solitude, where he would need protection, where Brother Patrick Hart could act as his secretary, and where I could act as his shield, keeping people away from him and even keeping him from wanting too much contact with the world, once he had again tasted it.

The reason that Eastern spirituality interested Merton was because monastic spirituality has its roots in the same soil in which the Eastern spirituality has its roots. This is not completely the same as what we're familiar with in Western spirituality, at least from St. Ignatius of Loyola and St. Francis De Sales and the more modern spiritualists. But if you live the monastic life and study it and try to enter it, and then read the Eastern Zen men and the Sufis and people like that, you find an awful lot of things that help you to understand your own tradition, your own monastic tradition. Merton was also convinced that it was the time for humanity and for educated men in the East and West to know one another better. He said somewhere, I think in print, that it's no longer proper that men going to college in America expose themselves to the Greek and Roman classics but not to the Hindu classics and the Buddhist classics.

And now to that day, December 10, 1968.

About 10 A.M. I received a phone call from the State Department in Washington. The message was very brief, to the point. Merton was dead and they wanted me to be informed; no details or anything like that. Well, I was shocked, and I took some time out and made a visit to the chapel and said a few prayers and took a walk around the monastery and came back to my office. And about fifteen minutes later, maybe a half-hour, I went into the adjoining office of the secretary, as I do several times a day. I presumed I had myself fairly well composed by then. He said to me, before I said anything, "What's wrong?" So that meant my facial expression was saying more than I had intended.

Eventually, I got through to the embassy in Bangkok and they confirmed it and they said there had been an accidental death; no more than that. I asked for an autopsy because I wanted to have answers to questions I knew would be coming. So then we called in Patrick Hart as we wanted to inform all of Father Louis's friends before they heard it in the public announcements. And it was Brother Patrick who was the first one to really break down, he just collapsed in the chair and wept when he heard it. It was a very painful period for all of us. He was a beloved man. He was our Father Louis, not so much the world's Thomas Merton.

By the time we got the body back, which took about a week, we were more or less ready for the funeral, to sing the Alleluias and think about him being in a better life and things like that. But it was a great loss to me, . . . I thought he had a lot more that he could do. And one of the reasons I accepted the office of abbot was that Merton would be one of my chief advisors.

I eventually went to Bangkok, in 1971, to see for myself exactly where he died, and I visited the Red Cross Center. They have a large hall and bungalows around it, with room for four people, two downstairs and two upstairs. Father Louis was downstairs in the particular bungalow he was in. Because of Thai superstition (as I heard it) they will never use that room again as a sleeping room, because someone died in there the way he did, accidentally. So they use it only as a speaking room. And the Catholic nuns who go there for their retreat conferences use it because it was used by Merton and is where Merton died. So if that keeps up, the tradition keeps up—we'll always know which of these otherwise identical bungalows was Merton's. Which I think is kind of a nice sort of memorial.

But there is much more than an empty room that he left behind. Everyone sees him differently, but Thomas Merton for me was a spiritual master, and I would say that he's the most extraordinary spiritual master that I've met, a living master. I've met others who were very good men, who had a certain amount of prudence, a certain amount of spirituality, but I felt that Merton was a true spiritual master. And I think this is documented in his writings. And I believe that people will read Thomas Merton's spiritual writings as long as they're reading John of the Cross's writings or *The Cloud of Unknowing* or Augustine. The men and women of our day, I think, can find a very, very deep and sophisticated statement of spiritual life, and spiritual realities in the writings of Thomas Merton. I really think that that's the part of his legacy that will last forever. His political thoughts are good, especially in so far as they're prophetic. But they'll be dated, and his thoughts about monastic renewal will be dated. Writings about the Church and the liturgy, they're already dated, being pre-Vatican II.

Some ask if he was a man who wrestled with God; was it a struggle for him, or a great love affair? Well, I believe that it was simply the consciousness of God and God's purpose in the world that permeated Merton's personality and his writings, and I think this was why he was autobiographical in his nature. He realized himself to be a divine mystery; God created him, God had called him into being. He had divine meaning, and he was existential enough to grapple with this in his own person and his own life. I think that's why he's so attractive to most people, because people can feel an affinity with that. They realize that he's not just talking for himself. I've had many, many people tell me that they read such and such in Merton, and they say, "That's not Merton, that's me; that's my own life."

Many people speak to me about Merton and admit they are

envious because I knew him on a personal basis. And while I'm very happy that I did know him, I always felt the deeper part of Merton he revealed only in his books. It would be actually impossible for him to reveal himself as intimately to most people as he does in his books. I suspect it's too intimate, those things that pertain to your relationship to God. I suppose if you could speak of it easily, you wouldn't have much to say. Maybe I read things into his books because of my personal knowledge of him, which other people can't get, but I think they are very fine points. His thought is accessible to everyone.

Others ask, "Will Merton be declared a saint someday?" I think Merton's own idea of a saint was a person who was completely aware of his need for God's mercy, a person with the self-knowledge that you don't become a saint on your own, God makes you a saint. That you have to be willing to let him do it and own up to your own poverty. And according to that definition of a saint, I think he was a saint. He was a person who was very conscious of his need for God's mercy, his sinfulness, his weakness. And I don't think he was in for any surprises when he came before the Lord on Judgment Day. Most of us, I think, have a little surprise in store for us when we come before the clarity of God and see ourselves. We'll have some experience of chagrin. But I suspect that Merton had already seen that and had placed that before the Lord and depended on him to take care of it, which is evident all through his books—that we are saved by the mercy of God

It occurred to me, looking back on my long relationship with Merton, that he had proved me either a liar or a foolish young man. After he died, as Abbot of Gethsemani, I had the opportunity or the necessity of becoming a spokesman for him, to explain what he stood for. And I realized that when I related what I held about the monastic life and about spiritual life and then what Merton held, that they were the same thing. Obviously he didn't get it from me. So I realized that actually I did become a disciple of Merton, willy nilly, in God's providence.

John Eudes Bamberger

So yesterday, I made my solemn vows. . . . I was left with a profoundly clean conviction that I had done the right thing and that I have given myself as best I could to God. . . . I am part of Gethsemani. I belong to the family. It is a family about which I have no illusions. —*The Sign of Jonas*

John Eudes Bamberger was a physician when he entered Our Lady of Gethsemani in 1950, as a novice under Thomas Merton. After profession and ordination as a priest, he studied psychiatry in Washington and theology in Rome. In 1971, he was elected abbot of Our Lady of Genesee, a monastery founded by Gethsemani, near Rochester, New York. There he continues to reside in his monastic community.

The monastic vocation is mysterious, often even to the monk himself. As an abbot I speak to many people who see me when they think they have a vocation, and one finds there as many different stories as there are people. But there are some common threads in them, the most frequent being some experience that causes a man to perceive himself and his life in quite a new light. And once one sees that way he is an inhabitant of another world and begins looking for a way to realize the values he sees from that new perspective. A certain number of people happen to live near a monastery or have known a monk, or somebody who had made a retreat to a monastery. And for some reason it strikes them that maybe that's where they could find what life is about now, having had this new kind of experience. The monastic life appeals to people who have had some awakening that makes them feel that living in a way that doesn't go to the heart of life is a waste of time. Its biggest appeal is that the monastic life encourages and facilitates a man's living at his own frontier.

I think that for Thomas Merton the experience of being forgiven by God was one of his deepest experiences, and I don't think he ever forgot that. It wouldn't appear normally because usually he gave the impression of being a rather carefree, happy-go-lucky, freewheeling type of person. And he was. He had a striking and infectious sense of humor; he was very human and very available. But when you knew him well—and you had to know him well to see this—there always was this awareness that he had been very bad off at one time. He would indicate this at times by some sudden word, some touching sign of sympathy that was spontaneous and simple. It is a fact that quite early he was all but homeless for all practical purposes. Prior to entering the monastery he felt he had lost his human innocence, and he could not feel he deserved compassion because of having been too violent in his ways with people, too selfish or greedy. He had, just as he had a passion for spiritual beauty later on, a very passionate nature for all kinds of things. And he'd indulged it too much. But he never totally identified with that: he always believed in innocence, I think. And somehow he was able, because of the experience of God, to believe that God had recreated his innocence. God gave him compassion, and that made the difference.

I think it began, as he says in *The Seven Storey Mountain,* when he went to Rome. He went as a tourist and became a pilgrim. He had two very profound experiences there. One in his hotel room one night when his father, who had died not so very long before, was suddenly in the room with him. His father had been an artist and developed cancer of the brain and couldn't talk the last time Merton saw him at the hospital. But he was drawing little figures, Byzantine saints, symbols of a profound religious faith at a time when Merton had none. Somehow, knowing his father was still alive, was spiritually present, began to change him; you can't have that kind of experience without coming alive yourself in some transcendent way.

And then when he continued his stay in Rome, he began visiting the churches, the basilicas in Rome, many of which have Byzantine mosaics in them. Cosmas and Damian was one that he visited.

And in standing before them as a tourist and an esthete, the religious content of those mosaics began to influence him.

I think it was a gradual thing, but I think too he had an encounter with God and he sensed that God knew him at his worst and his best, and that God loved him. I think Merton's deepest sense of who he was, was that he was a sinner whom God had found and forgiven and made a son. I don't think he was so bad in his youth, but he sensed it as so bad after he had a series of experiences, beginning in Rome, of a very pure vision of God and man. He came to recognize it as a very elevated and high call and that he had been unfaithful to God. He knew too that he should have responded better when he was younger, but didn't. And he therefore judged himself by a very high standard.

He had to do it in this fashion; he was a very dramatic type of person. He had very profound insights that for him were more real than the stones in a wall. They were concrete, God was concrete for him.

My own relationship with him began with the reading of *The Seven Storey Mountain* when I was a junior in medical school. I was very impressed by the book, chiefly because it spoke to me about an experience of God, and it did in a way that seemed very human. But at the time I had no intention at all of becoming a monk. I went on and became a physician. But I was living a life of prayer, and as I started to become more serious about my faith, earlier when I was in the Navy, then later on when working as an intern, it became apparent I should become a monk.

I was accepted at Gethsemani in 1950, and I was rather mystified by what I found there, because my only contact with the monastery was through reading this book. At that time Gethsemani was growing tremendously. They had sent out a group in 1949 to found Mepkin, and in 1951 founded Genesee. They had to make new foundations because there were so many new people coming in, so many in fact that there were fifty men who lived in a tent, all year round. And so there was a lot of life and young people and enthusiasm, not just high natural feelings, but enthusiasm for the ideal, for a life lived with God. Gethsemani in those days was very poor and simple; for example, we used horses instead of tractors for our work in the fields and the forests. I remember plowing with a horse-drawn plow, and we used horses to haul wood from the forest. It was a very simple and austere life then.

For Americans, it was a bit difficult to, first of all, get up at two in the morning. When you first began that seemed austere, but after you did it long enough it seemed quite natural. You did get enough sleep but it didn't feel like it to begin with. But I think the silence was the chief austerity. To live in silence without any chatting, that was difficult. The monastic rule is that you never just chat, that you only speak when it's important or at least helpful, and you speak only to a few designated people. And we lived that pretty well.

The lifestyle was very simple, and the silence tended to make it very intense. And there weren't too many emotional outlets. But it had as its rationale that one had to discover inner ways, the inner path, and discover the inner light, and focus on creating a life where emotions were increasingly invested in your relationsihp with the Lord in prayer. And once you caught on to that, gradually it seemed less and less austere.

After I was there for a little while, I began to wonder which one of these people could be the one who wrote that book. And then one day we had a lecture by Father Louis, as we called Merton there, but I never would have picked him out to be the one. He was a very different type than the image he projected in his writings. He was a very outgoing person with an obvious ease with relationships, very approachable, with a great sense of humor. He had tremendous energy and dynamism. Almost anything that he took a liking to he became enthusiastic about, very quickly, as I learned as the years went on. But that wasn't the impression his books gave. His books give the impression of a person who was on top of things, and who had a very involved but balanced vision.

There was a great openness about him and yet a concealed reserve, too. At times one would be aware that he was going through a considerable struggle about some aspect or other of life, because he was inclined not to hide it; that was a part of his way. He'd express some complaint about our work, for example, or the dryness of long periods in the choir. He felt you should let it all come out, not wrap your cowl around you and submerge. Yet, he was very reticent to talk about the deepest things. . . . For example, his experience with prayer. You'll find there was nothing directly stated about that in any of his writings or on any of his tapes.

But in personal terms, he didn't worry too much about what might happen if he said what he felt and thought. Or what impression it might give, and I think that was part of his mystique at Gethsemani. He felt that you did what you must, and life would eventually correct itself. If you did that with whatever seemed real when it came up, then you'd eventually be more true and complete as a man.

If you knew him, Merton had a great deal of spontaneous joy and humor but, like so many people who are inclined that way at times, when he was down it was heavy. He seemed to me to be unfair at those times in critical remarks he might make. I can remember meeting him out in the woods when his bearing exuded a heavy melancholy. And if you're at all a sensitive person you can pick it up when people are down, and I could certainly see that he was. I knew him fairly well, we lived together eighteen years, and one gets to know the moods and the changes of a person's personality pretty well. But that was uncommon; usually he came through as being full of energy and enthusiasm.

He could be very abrupt when he chose to be. He had no trouble letting you know that you were staying too long, or taking too much of his time. But he had developed this in a way that wasn't objectionable, it was just very clear that he meant it, that you should get out now. It was not his usual way. He had a kind of spontaneous sympathy that's really very rare. Especially if you were going through a hard period, he would pick it up very quickly and respond to it with a profound intensity that was not just a formal monastic reaction. He really was very responsive to human suffering.

A great deal has been said about Merton, and the whole problem of authority and struggles with obedience and his superiors in the order—Dom James Fox in particular, who was his abbot for some twenty years. It's important to put that in the context of a monastic vocation. One of the chief things you have to confront when you become a monk is the whole question of obeying a superior. St. Benedict says a monk is someone who wants to be under an abbot. But that's pretty tricky because it doesn't lead to God unless you're also free. Cistercian spirituality centers on freedom, because it's concerned with love and you can never force love. Obedience, then, is a challenge to honesty, to integrity, and to meekness. And if you don't become freer by the way you obey, it's probably better not to be a monk. That's a pretty high order for all of us.

There were periods when Merton felt that the abbot was too narrow. I think he also felt that he was being used at times. Actually, the whole problem with censorship and Merton that is talked about so much—the abbot had nothing to do with that. That came from higher authorities in the church and rippled down to the order. In the end, Merton told Ernesto Cardenal in a letter (May 10, 1965) that he published about all he really wanted to.

I think the relationship between Merton and Dom James Fox not only began well, I think it ended well, but there were rough periods in between. We can't forget that for many, many years Merton saw his abbot every week, discussing his work and so on. He also acted as the abbot's spiritual director for a long period, and they were very open with one another. That just doesn't happen unless there is something positive going on year after year.

It was a very human relationship, and Merton wasn't happy all the time. But there were periods when I think Merton would have been extremely difficult for anyone to deal with, partly because he *did* have special insights. He often saw things before they were very clear to anyone else. For example, at the very beginning of the atomic arms issue, he saw its implications; he was one of the first people in the country to foresee the way Vietnam would go;

he predicted the race violence in the United States a couple years before the blood flowed. He wanted active responses on these issues, while others didn't see them that way. When you're an abbot you can't just think of only the person you're dealing with, you have to think of the way a decision or course of action will influence others or be perceived by others, and sometimes even for the sake of the monk himself who wants to do something. I run across this at least every week in dealing with monks, and I think anyone who has a sizable group of people that he's responsible for is often in that position, not excluding parents and schoolteachers.

Merton often felt that his views were really very clear and obvious and was prepared to fight for them. He believed in them, and he did have a lot of courage. And so at times that was hard to handle. If you didn't see it the way he did, and he felt he was right, and you treated it like it was not all that important—it didn't take too much imagination to see that tension would arise.

I think dealing with Merton was more challenging in many ways because of both his background and temperament. He was a man who had a deep need to know that he was appreciated and loved; it was very strong, I think stronger than average, much stronger than average. One reason he felt there was tension between him and the community after he moved to the hermitage, I'd think, was simply the fact that there was markedly reduced contact and so little opportunity for those small, daily signs of friendliness and acceptance that are important. He needed that. But, at the same time, he was a very independent type, I think partly because he had to be. His mother died when he was six, and his father was an artist who would suddenly decide to go off to North Africa to paint for a long period and leave his son behind. So he had to become emotionally free, probably more than he should have had to be as a young boy.

I think part of his extraverted ways was an expression of that need to be appreciated, to be loved, as perhaps he never had been. That's where he was complex. He also needed silence and solitude but when he was in a crowd he was very quickly the center. Even if people didn't know who he was. For example, one day there was a forest fire at Gethsemani, and we went out to fight the fire. After it was over, a group wound up several miles away from the monastery, waiting for a car to come and pick us up. Merton was in that group and we went into a general store in a little town in Kentucky where a bunch of high school kids had come in after school. In just a few minutes all the kids were around Merton, listening to him. He knew how to speak to them in their language, and he had them in the palm of his hand, fascinated by this monk.

There is a certain amount of grumbling within a monastery at times, but I think Merton probably grumbled more than just average. He had needs and interests that very few people could have sustained for any length of time. And he frequently experienced our shortcomings as personal frustrations. We were a pretty ordinary group of people, and he was extraordinary in many ways. He had strong feelings about certain things that we weren't sensitive to, and I think sometimes we disappointed him. And he wasn't the type to always keep to himself—he let it show.

I think at times our emphasis on the relatively unimportant details of life bothered him. Not being clearly committed enough to the contemplative life. Getting too involved with work or cheese or rules. He had very high ideals and unusual gifts and I think special grace from God, and it took a lot to measure up to what he felt life should provide and express. And most of us just didn't have it, perhaps none of us did. But he judged himself by the same standards, and he could laugh at himself too. He wasn't always easy to put up with either, and he knew it.

I think that, late in his life, Merton was quite weary of community life, and he was probably grumbling more than usual. I personally have an opinion about that period that I've never seen anyone express. When Merton became a hermit, it was very important to him because he was gifted for prayer and solitude and silence. But I myself believe that he was not quite suited to be a hermit. He was never able to face that, and I believe that instead of facing it he took it out on the community. That may sound defensive, because I was part of that community, but I think there's a lot of evidence for that, and I believe when the evidence is out that that will be quite clear. Although he was sour on the community at times, I never saw that he was bitter. Other people have felt that he was, but I think I knew Merton probably as well as anyone because I was his physician for a long time, and I saw him at his worst physically, and often emotionally. And I never saw him bitter. I often saw him distressed, but when you would pin him down on things he was a man of very deep faith, and he was tough.

It was part of his mystique to be outspoken, to say very strongly what he felt, but it's important to note that it didn't mean that he entirely believed everything he said in the heat of passion. There was a period when his political and social views were much more advanced than ours, and he felt a great disappointment in the community. But as he said later, he was taking things out on the community that were conflicts within himself. He saw it very differently later and, as he says in his *Asian Journal,* he never wanted to be separated from the community. He probably didn't think it was prudent to go back to the hermitage after the trip. He thought he might live elsewhere but he wanted to live and die as a monk of the community.

Merton also had various health problems toward the and of his life that bothered him a lot. I remember one day he came up to me in the infirmary—it was during his period as a hermit when he used to chop wood—and he told me he had a numbness in his hand. I thought that he might have a cervical disc impingement and sent him into the hospital. And that it was. It didn't respond well to conservative treatment so he required surgery for that, which is painful. He had other continuing ailments, stomach problems, digestive problems, and some allergies. Why did he have those things? That's kind of mysterious. Was it part of the tension that came with his struggles? But that wasn't the usual picture. In my years at Gethsemani, his health problems were pretty much in the background, except for a couple of brief periods and toward 1966 and 1967 during his hermit period—I think that's significant —his health was worse.

In December 1968, I was giving a retreat to the Conyers community down in Georgia when I received a call from Dom Flavian. "Father Louis has died in Bankgkok," he announced quietly. I was, of course, numbed by the message. I was told to cut the retreat short and come back because the body was to be flown into Louisville, and since I was the physician there I should be there to receive the body. He was fifty-three years old and was very much alive the last time I saw him, full of energy and enthusiasm as usual, and his death came as quite a shock. I think all of us who knew him well felt we had lost a brother; it was like losing somebody from the family. But on the other hand it came at a good time for him, because he had faced the deep conflicts he had been struggling with for an extended period and he had worked them through. I felt that if he had died suddenly it was fortunate it was not six months earlier or a year later. And from that point of view I felt that his death expressed a good deal of continuity with his monastic life, in the sense that he had resolved some of the tensions about his vocation.

When Merton died in Thailand, it was during the Vietnam War, so the Army had a team there who took care of Americans who died overseas in that part of Asia. His body was prepared by the Army for shipping back to the States, and was transferred to a civilian plane in San Francisco. A small group of monks—Abbot Flavian Burns; the cellarer, Brother Frederick; and I—met the plane and took the body back to the monastery, going through New Haven, Kentucky, where our undertaker is located. There we opened the coffin and the abbot and I both saw the body. I identified it and, because I felt that somebody would question whether it was Merton, I made a kind of official note at that time. And I kept that note so that there would be some evidence that it was indeed Merton's body. And sure enough, within a year someone had written that it wasn't Merton's body at all, he was alive someplace else.

My work for our order has taken me all over the world, to Africa, Latin America, Asia, and Europe, and I continue to see people who are interested in Merton and people who continue to write about him. I believe the reason is that Thomas Merton spoke about God in a very human way, in a way that was very convincing, because he wrote from experience and from full humanity. So as one reads Merton's accounts of various aspects of the spiritual life or monastic life, I think one has somewhat of a feeling that "Merton understands what I want to be, or what I would like to be, or what I'm trying to be, or what I've gone through, or what I'm coping with."

His books reach so many people because of this profound contact he had with his own depths. He had worked through a great deal of his own struggles with the emotional demands of life with God, and he knew himself very concretely as a result of the various demands that the life of prayer made on his humanity. And he suffered from it, but he didn't just endure it with a long face. He really absorbed it, and it made him very sensitive to what people had to go through to be a full human person, and to find who they are before God, to sustain what's best in them. I believe that, having done that, he developed a very profound compassion for the poor and for the oppressed, and for those who were pushed around. It made him a bit oversensitive at times—to authority, for instance—but that was perhaps the price to be paid.

I believe myself that Merton's early works, both his spiritual and his autobiographical writings, will be read as long as there are people who are interested in God and the experience of God. I think, even as human documents the earlier writings will stand up much better than the later ones. But who knows his place in the Church or what history will make of him? To me he certainly was a holy person, and I always thought there was something outstanding about Merton and his relationship with God. And even, at times, something heroic. A man of his sensitivity and gifts and intensity, I think, came up against pretty ultimate situations much more frequently than we who are more sedate and average. And although he went through some bad patches—as we say down in Kentucky—he basically remained faithful to his call, under a lot of stress at times, and he persevered in seeking God and in obedience.

The contemplative life encounters each of us at the point where we are most fully ourselves but also uncertain of who we really are. And so it's always a challenge, and I think that was why it stayed alive for Merton. He was wrestling with God, and there was always more to God than he could ever master. He felt that very deeply, and only someone who was heroic would have persevered and been faithful.

Jean Leclercq

The life is difficult, no doubt, but the faith and self-sacrifice which make it possible also fill the heart of the monk with a peace which the world cannot give. —*The Silent Life*

Jean Leclercq was born in 1911. At the age of sixteen, he asked to be admitted to the Benedictine Abbey at Clervaux, Luxembourg— as a lay brother, because he did not feel his was a vocation to the priesthood. But, after military service as an artillery gunner, he did begin studies for the priesthood and was ordained in 1936. Among his many scholarly works on medieval spirituality and monastic history, his voluminous writings on St. Bernard of Clairvaux, the father of the Cistercians, are considered the most comprehensive ever undertaken. He travels extensively to further monastic ecumenism.

I met Merton in a rather simple way. In the late 1940s I wrote to the Gethsemani library to get some information on their beautiful collection of manuscripts. The librarian bid me welcome. His name was Father Louis. I suppose he was doing almost everything at that time. So we started a correspondence.

Early in our letters I took the opportunity to criticize his *The Sign of Jonas,* which I hadn't read but knew was a diary. I said, "A monk should never speak of himself." And he kindly accepted my rather rough dismissal but he said, "How much I would give to have the diary of Bernard of Clairvaux in the twelfth century." I was not convinced at the time, but later I was in an African monastery, and I heard *The Sign of Jonas* read. Everybody was not only edified, but pleased and instructed and inspired. Yes, he was doing valuable work, I thought to myself; "I am being too narrow." And in fact our correspondence became always more intense and regular, and whenever I came to America I went to visit him.

Although Merton wanted to read about Bernard's life eight centuries later, I don't think he himself was writing so that people in the future would know what monastic life was like today. He was thinking of the present. First, he was a writer, and he had a certain need to write; it didn't matter too much on what. But he was a monk, and he knew there were so many strange ideas on monastic life, that it was a refuge for sadness, or extreme austerity, and things like that. So he wanted to react against the myths and to show the reality as he found it himself. He was a very happy man.

In the monastic life, there are two aspects. There is the external —what you do, why, at what time, with what people, and so forth. And observances, work, liturgy. Then there is the interiority—the spiritual experience. And that is what matters. So always Merton gave less importance to all the externals. He concentrated on the core of monastic life, which was essentially prayer—communion with God, the search for God. And the best he wrote, I think, were the books and essays and articles in which he spoke of that. Not his writings on political or social involvement. I think of two of his books: *Seeds of Contemplation,* which was completed by *New Seeds of Contemplation;* and one of the books published after his death—*The Climate of Monastic Prayer.* These two are classics. In *Seeds* he wrote on the theory and showed practical examples of how to pray; whereas in *Climate* he considered more the environment, the importance of silence.

He is surely the man who brought this word *contemplation* back to our vocabularies, but it is a difficult word, for there is no possible definition of *contemplation.* It is a bit frightening, because in these days it seems to indicate some sure path through the various states of mystical life. I prefer to use "contemplative prayer." And that was what Merton always advocated. He was not preaching certain states of high mystical life, but a capacity, an easiness to be in dialogue with God, or just listening without talking in silence, to be in attention to God. It's a matter of love, not just a psychological activity.

Merton experienced that simple, mysterious contact with God and wrote about it. But he reached so many people who don't live in monasteries because he showed to those people that the reality of prayer is not the monopoly of a rarefied species living in cloisters, in some sort of a romantic setting and out of the real conditions of life. Everybody can't pray that way. There are conditions that favor contemplative prayer, but those are only a matter of climate, of exterior environment, of praying times in the liturgy. To Merton, the object of prayer was eventually to enjoy God. Not as a personal enjoyment, pleasure, satisfaction, but to be with him. Whether you speak or are silent, to be with him.

Now, that's mysterious, difficult to explain, but you can evoke it if you've experienced it. And that is where Merton the poet has something to contribute. A professor could maybe explain contemplative prayer in clear terms—I don't know whether he would convince anybody. But the poet can evoke that with images and beauty—and that was the single reason why Merton was and still is read so much. Not only because his books are beautifully written—any professional writer can learn how to present correct and beautiful copy—no—he had a style that was so simple, so imaginative, so poetic that everybody could understand it. Everybody could identify with the style of Merton.

I remember myself, in the beginning when I didn't read much of him and I began to meet so many people in Europe who adopted the Christian faith or the monastic life after reading *The Seven Storey Mountain* or another of his books. "But how did it happen?" The answer was "Well, I read his book, and I discovered that was my story. His story was my story. So I identified with him and I went all the way with him."

As you try to place Merton among spiritual fathers of the church and spiritual writers, you find that he would be among the poets, along the lines of Bernard, John of the Cross, and Gregory of Nyssa. They were writers full of images, because they were full of the Bible. Like them, Merton was both unique and traditional. *Traditional* does not mean merely to repeat. *Traditional* means to transmit, to convey the message, and to do it efficiently you have to renew it. To just repeat, you are a professor, you know everything that has been said before—but that does not contribute. So what Merton did was assimilate all the tradition and then to reexpress it in his own style.

What struck me in my long correspondence with Merton was his continuous eagerness to know about the monastic life. He was not a scholar, not an historian; he was an expert in nothing. And he knew it, and he didn't want to be. He didn't want to play the game of an expert. But he was always inquiring about new texts, new publications, asking me to send him books and articles, to tell him about my studies. I've spent my life studying monastic history and therefore tradition, but in the living sense, and he always stressed that. Living tradition.

So here was a man, very modern yet steeped in tradition, living a traditional life. It was predictable that such a man would have, how do you say, "personality conflicts." Dom James Fox and Thomas Merton (Father Louis), they were both great personalities at Gethsemani. And because of that, they were different; otherwise they would have been average people and with no problems—just agreeing on everything. No. Dom James was in the Navy before, then a Trappist, and very soon he was elected as abbot because he was very intelligent and had qualities of spiritual discernment. But he was responsible for a corporation at a time when there were rather strict regulations, so he had to keep the whole thing going as it had been going for centuries—that was his job.

Now Merton was a free man. A very good Trappist, he joined with joy and he swallowed everything—at the beginning. After a few years he started asking, "Why that, why this?" Not to destroy, not even to criticize, but just to try to justify.

Dom James was not a man caught in the past; he was caught in the present. And, although this is hard to see at the time, the institution to which he belonged was just starting to evolve. It was evolving very slowly, and Merton wanted it to evolve more rapidly, not so much at the level of the usages or even institutions, but of mentality. He wanted to introduce maybe more culture, more awareness of other cultures, other religious traditions. Merton was not an expert, but he was a sort of genius: he had a greater capacity to assimilate everything and to retransmit in simple, understandable ways.

So he wanted to bring some new air. And the proof that he deserved to be the conveyor of the Trappist tradition—even while these two men had their conflicts—was that he was appointed by Dom James novice master. So during about ten years he was in charge of precisely conveying the tradition.

To be sure, it was not easy to be the abbot of Merton. And for Merton it was not easy to be the monk of a great and strong personality like Fox. The point on which there was the greatest conflict at a certain time was—and that's the second most important item in our correspondence—his vocation to solitude. Merton wanted to find a form of solitary life but within the institution that he had chosen, that he loved, in which he wanted to stay. So, at the first, it was apparent that it was impossible; Fox would not allow it. So Merton dreamed of going elsewhere, either to Europe or Mexico or in this country. But then, progressively, both Dom James and Merton came to consider this and I intervened a bit because I wrote various things on hermit life. Then they found the ideal solution of building this beautiful small hermitage on the grounds so Merton could come every day to the community. He came every day at the end of the morning for Mass and lunch, and Dom James sometimes said that was because he hated to cook or to wash the dishes. But then Merton also came every Sunday afternoon and gave a talk. Nobody ever knew about what it would be—an ancient monastic author, a Marxist philosopher, a Japanese poet, whatever. It was always a surprise, and that was what Merton added to Gethsemani—his capacity to absorb everything and to convey it.

Last winter, on the occasion of moving the Trappist General House in Rome from one place to another, about fifty letters or more were discovered, letters from Merton to his abbot general, Dom Gabriel Sortais. And, of course, they didn't write to say nothing. There must have been something important for Merton to write about; first, I suppose the evolution of the institution; then his own problem, his own vocation. So we have to keep a certain prudence when we pronounce anything before they are published. Also twenty letters or so, important long letters, spiri-

tual letters to a nun in England have been discovered. So all of that
will have to be inserted in his biography.

Just a little bit about Bangkok and how Merton came to be with
us. It is a divine mystery how he came and then to die there.
Monsignor Jean Jadot had just been appointed the first nuncio to
Thailand and that area, and he came to see me in Clervaux just
after his consecration. We wanted a meeting of our group, Aid to
Implantation of Monasteries (AIM), and I suggested Bangkok.
Then I said, right away; "Why don't we invite Thomas Merton to
give some *brio* to our meeting, and also to bring his message?"
The idea was accepted, and the invitation was sent to Gethsemani,
and Merton agreed. He said it would be interesting, and by that
time Dom Flavian had become abbot, so there was a new way.
And Merton was free to travel.

When we laid out the program, I thought it was essential to
have something said about Marxism in Asia . . . we were next
door to Vietnam and Cambodia, and so everyone was wondering
about monasticism in that context. So I asked him to speak on
that, and he immediately answered, "Yes, I have become familiar
this year with Marcuse and so I'm ready to see the similarities and
differences. You know, these Marxists have something to tell us."
He said in this letter that "the purpose of monasticism is not sur-
vival, but prophecy." And he added, "We are all busy saving our
skins, that seems to be our highest priority." Anyway, that's how
he prepared that talk, which I didn't hear and I didn't read. The
very morning when he was going to give his paper I went out to
stretch my legs. I saw a pagoda, I went in, I met a monk who
spoke English, he invited me to their one meal a day, a long meal.
And then I visited everything, I attended the investiture of a young
monk. And when I came back at the end of the morning for the
Eucharist, the talk was over, so I was not there for this big show-
ering of applause for Thomas Merton.

The last thing I heard from him was the day before when I had
been charged to introduce all the participants. I said, "I suppose I
have been asked to do this because I am the AIM clown." And so

I said, "I have invited my friend Father Louis Merton to help me, in view of my poor English." And he said, "We shall clown together." That's the last word I heard of him—"We shall clown together." The next day he gave his paper and said at the end, "Now, I shall disappear." That was prophecy.

I think his legacy has been to call attention to the importance of prayer in life. Not so much prayer as an activity, as an obligation, a particular exercise, but a prayer life. To be a pray-er. Each one according to his environment. And that the monastic setup was a very favorable, but not the only, condition for that. Merton also showed there was no need for a dichotomy or tension between the facts of being in solitude and being universal. Often the people who are the less busy in a particular thing are the more available to universal concerns. Merton was a perfect example of that. The more alone he was, the more his horizons were open. So I think Merton showed that it's for ordinary people to have a real prayer life and to be committed to universal concerns at all the levels. Maybe some of the positions he took in his time are not relevant, but the tendency to be in prayer in a life of action is a lasting message of Merton.

Richard Loomis

The more I get to know my scholastics the more reverence I have for their individuality and the more I meet them in my own solitude. . . . Their calmness will finally silence all that remains of my own turbulence.

—*The Sign of Jonas*

Richard Loomis was a Trappist monk at Our Lady of Gethsemani from 1949 to 1953. He is married, father of two sons, and a professor of English at Nazareth College, Rochester, New York.

At the beginning of my days at Gethsemani, we young monks did our reading in the novices' scriptorium. It was a large, rather austere room where we sat on benches along the walls and would keep one or two books that we had *ad usum,* that is, for personal use, in a little box beneath our seats. Though the room had a small shelf of religious books, it was nothing like the libraries we know outside. Later, as scholastics, when we were to have group conferences with Thomas Merton, who was then master of scholastics we were ushered into a vault that had been converted to serve as his study. To us, it was a taste of the world outside! This room was lined with books, and they weren't just old books. Merton's was a collection of books dealing with a whole range of topics, and they were mostly modern books, fiction as well as theology. We were there not to gape at the books on the wall, but to listen to what he had to tell us. But you couldn't help but notice them. And for me the immediate association was with those apartments where books line the walls, as I'd seen in places like San Francisco, where I had met people who led an intense intellectual and artistic life. This environment was part of the experience of coming to listen to Thomas Merton. It certainly had a different flavor from the more traditional rooms in the monastery.

I can't remember a lot of specific lessons that he taught so much as I remember certain things he said that reflected an attitude that was distinctive. For example, on one occasion, he made an allusion to some of the books that were on his shelves, books by William Faulkner. This was the early 1950s, and Merton talked about Faulkner being down there in Mississippi, just staying in Oxford, writing his novels. He called it "a wonderful contemplative life." That registered, not just because it was an allusion to a contemporary author, but because something was being suggested: first, that Thomas Merton might have liked to go down there and be William Faulkner. He could see fulfilling his vocation by living in a quiet southern town and just devoting himself to his resources as a native of that region. And second, the notion of seeing a modern novelist as leading a kind of contemplative life—this idea has borne fruit in my thinking over the years, as I've seen more and more the closeness between the artist's vocation and the contemplative's. And of course Thomas Merton had both vocations.

The first dealings I had with Thomas Merton—or Father Louis, as we knew him—was when he served as hebdomadary priest: a weekly assignment that included celebrating the community Mass and supervising the serving of food at the tables in the refectory. All the novices, as well as the professed, sat on one side of the tables and on the other side the servers moved up and down. The hebdomadary priest supervised this, which meant he actually came around and offered you cornbread or oil and vinegar. The Trappists do without so many things that for them to practice any kind of individual self-restraint means moderating the amount of coffee that they take or whether or not they will put some oil and vinegar on their vegetables. But the way Merton offered the oil and vinegar always said, "Go ahead and put some oil and vinegar on those vegetables. Don't do without it." Oh yes, he could do that kind of small service with grace and good humor. He was also a good worker in the fields. There were certain occasions when the whole community would go out and work together, and I can still see his figure marching off to hack down trees or whatever, and being one of those who really put his back to it.

He bore the monastic name of Father Louis, but it wasn't just a name that distinguished him from the published author Thomas Merton. He was a priest, a teacher, that's what we saw within the community. The fact that he was writing books that were getting published was a mysterious activity that somehow got accomplished. When, as a young professed monk, I got admitted to his study, I had some better idea of how he got that work done. But in earlier days, when he was writing *The Seven Storey Mountain,* he did his typing on an old typewriter in an unheated scriptorium, and his fingers nearly froze. He got his work done whether or not he had comfortable facilities. But you didn't see that ordinarily, you saw him in all those other roles—for example, as hebdomadary priest. And it wasn't for Thomas Merton that you might feel a certain respect, it was a liking for Father Louis, a member of the community who did these silent tasks, and did them nicely.

He was an exemplary monk. And given all the changes in monasticism that he became involved in, he always observed the Rule, and he did so with good spirit.

I'll never forget once in the Chapter of Faults—where anyone can call out anyone else's name and the person named has to prostrate himself and then listen to being charged with some fault or defect—I remember once being proclaimed by one of the younger monks who I always thought was a terrific fellow and who declared that my fault was that I was behaving too stiffly. It's not enough to be correct and formal in your bows, or in serving the oil, or whatever else you're doing in the monastic community. There's supposed to be a natural simplicity and warmth manifested. Well, that was something that Thomas Merton had by instinct.

When I would go to him for spiritual direction what I remember chiefly is the candor, the openness, and the tact with which he could conduct those sessions. For example, you could talk to him about emotional turbulence. Ordinarily, you didn't go into a confessional in a Trappist monastery and say, "Emotionally, I'm distraught." But you could talk very directly to him about that, and one reason was that he would say, "Yeah, yeah, I've had that too." And know what you're talking about. This is related to that element in him that was beautifully balanced and easy. And with all the unusual things that he had done and that he was doing at the monastery, that's what I most marvel at—that he could have kept that. Because it doesn't stay there unless you have a very good gyroscope.

He was a humble monk who obeyed the rules, but he certainly was also an innovator. Our abbot, Dom James Fox, was also a person of a progressive temperament. Dom James had a master's degree from the Harvard School of Business and would have been a tremendously sucessful and dynamic entrepreneur wherever he had gone. Father Louis could have pursued a host of professions with great success. And both of them would have been doing new things; things on the frontier of whatever career they'd chosen. And here they had chosen to sequester themselves in an isolated community. When Dom James went there and later when Father Louis went there, Gethsemani was by no means a celebrated, notorious place that a lot of people flocked to and that news stories were written about. It was a hidden-away community pursuing an ancient way of life that was as medieval as possible. So here you have the irony of progressive personalities deliberately choosing an archaic and secluded way of life that might seem to stand against any sort of creative and innovative career. Each of them, in fact, would have an opportunity to become innovative, because Dom James was able to preside over the expansion of the order, the founding of the new houses, the physical rebuilding of Gethsemani, and the beginning, in the 1950s, of those reforms that were to get a focus during the years of Vatican II.

Thomas Merton, besides being well-known to the outside world as a writer, could, within the monastery, be a master of kind gestures. I remember when I was about to leave the monastery, he reached into his desk and said, "Here's something to take with you." It was a tiny little bit of a dark brown thing encased in a kind of plastic container. Then he gave me the little certificate that authenticated it as a relic of St. Augustine, the doctor of the church. Some European prelate had given it to him, and he was giving this to me. At the time I simply accepted it, because it was very generous. But afterward I thought, "That's an extravagant kind of gift to give to someone who's merely going back to the world." And in fact, a couple of years later I was married and we had a couple of kids and were living in a tiny, crowded apartment, and the precious relic just got lost. Who knows whether one of the boys ate it or tossed it out the window? And that particular loss of a valuable little relic, which was also a gift from Thomas Merton, has lingered with me as an emblem of what sometimes happens to precious gifts. The gifts can get lost, but the generosity survives.

Though you leave the monastery, you can keep the unity of focus of the new life you've experienced there. I remember experiencing monastic generosity on my first retreat at Gethsemani, a year and a half before I joined the community. In those days, when you made a retreat, you were served at table by lay brothers who did not speak. And you were served a tremendous quantity of food, all farm fresh, and those loaves of thick, wonderful whole-wheat bread and farm butter. And you knew that the monks were living frugally. Their good temper and their generosity when serving you those magnificent meals conveyed an impression of a hospitality such as you find only in certain happy families and not in a lot of other places in the modern world. And that bespoke an ability to be generous while still practicing self-denial. Thomas Merton was generous and unselfish and open in just that way.

Maurice Flood

I have fallen into the great indignity I have written against—I am a contemplative who is ready to collapse from overwork. This, I think, is a sin and the punishment of sin but now I have got to turn it to good use and be a saint by it, somehow.   —*The Sign of Jonas*

Maurice Flood, forty eight, entered the Abbey of Our Lady of Gethsemani in 1957 and took his perpetual vows as a Trappist monk in 1965. His life as a brother within the order is a balance of prayer, work, and reading. Brother Maurice is now a monk at Holy Cross Abbey, Berryville, Virginia.

He had a nameplate on the outside of the door to the little library annex where he worked, and everyone knew who it was, so there was no mixup. "Uncle Louie," the sign read. That was the offhanded way he called himself, and so "Uncle Louie" brought out in us the same response you would give to any real, wholesome person; you want to help them. Somehow you know a person like this has his burdens and a lot to do, and so any little help you can give, you do. That's where I liked to fill in, typing manuscripts sometimes, or helping him bring some things to the hermitage. He had a bad back, so I carried wood to the hermitage. He had contaminated water for a while, so we carried jugs of water up to the hermitage.

He had his serious side and he worked hard, but if you ever listened to his tapes you'd get another aspect of Thomas Merton. There was always a lot of laughter in the background when he held conferences in the monastery. I called him a wholesome person. . . . some call people like that saints and mystics, but they're really earthly persons, down to earth, they radiate wholeness. They have this integration of the universe within them. The whole of creation—they hold that and they like to share it.

But he had to struggle like any of us. As the years passed, he was hovering around it and getting closer and then he gradually was pulled into the center, where there was no escape from what he called the wholesomeness of love, the center of love. Once you get in the center there is no return, no going out. It's scary and sometimes dark, but once you get in there you know that's where the center of life is. It's not a place, and it's hard to explain, but I think when people know what it's like there more people would want to make that journey too. He made the journey, and he let others know what it was like.

The idea of the monastic life is freeing oneself from illusion to embrace this centeredness in God, which we have received through the revelation of Jesus Christ. Sometimes it sounds very tedious and sort of ethereal but, when you live it, it becomes more and more defined. Gandhi, now there's another whole man. He had that mischievous twinkle and a teasing way about him even when he was in his very serious confrontations with the government. He knew that truth would win out no matter what would happen to him, and he had this really boyish way about him. He was free. Uncle Louie was like that.

I myself am the kind of person who would rather stay in the background and do what I can and not try too hard in being overbearing in wanting to know somebody. Sometimes, if you're just generous and don't come on so strong you get to know people easier that way. Merton usually ate his main meal at the monastery, and so when he would come down to the monastery we would have the Eucharist in a small chapel, just the two of us, and then we'd go to dinner in the main refectory. It was just the two of us offering the Eucharist, and those times were special, the couple of years we did that.

He came back to Gethsemani finally in a big casket. His body passed out of view, but he's been living in our hearts all this time. He's living in each of us now, and we are grateful for that. That's what gives us the courage and the strength, the buoyancy to go on, knowing that this man has gone before us.

V. MERTON THE PILGRIM

His Holiness, the Dalai Lama

It was a very warm and cordial discussion. And at the end, I felt we had become very good friends. And were somehow very close to each other. And I believe too, that there is a real spiritual bond between us.

—*The Asian Journal of Thomas Merton*

Gejong Tenzin Gyatsho, the fourteenth Dalai Lama, is the temporal and spiritual leader of six million Tibetans and the leader of additional millions of Mahayana Buddhists throughout Central Asia and the world. He received Thomas Merton at his residence-in-exile in Dharmsala, India in November 1968. Their lengthy sessions left such a lasting impression that His Holiness often refers to Merton in speeches and in his writings when he addresses the need for understanding between the nations and religions of the East and West.

Before I met him, this Thomas Merton, I had not much information about him. So we talked just in this same place and looked on each other's faces and expressed things, and with each word, each minute, there was deeper understanding.

I looked in his face. I could see a good human being. I don't know how to explain but . . . you can tell people who have some deep experience. And of course this is special. He was not the type of person who was cheating other people, or looking down at other people. Not like that kind at all. Honest. Truthful.

I could see he took a deep interest in Eastern philosophy, mainly Buddhism, and especially meditation. And he had an excellent understanding. He was very open-minded. That is good. Such a person, I think, was very useful in this period, when the West and East were just coming to know each other.

I always believed that it is very important, highly necessary, to develop a basic human feeling, or, how do you say, sort of a realization of oneness of all mankind. Different races, different ideologies, different religions are sometimes dividing, sometimes the source of conflict, of problems. But if you apply different religions, different philosophies, in the right way, all are same. A better human being, a good human being, good human community, happier human community—those are the goals. That largely depends on individual persons to see, and such a person was the late Thomas Merton. He was Christian, yes, but in the meantime very open-minded to take different religions' ideas and look at basically what they hope to achieve. Ah, yes, through him my understanding and my respect about other religions, particularly the Christian, was very much increased. Because of meeting with him I found many common practices between Christian monks and Buddhist monks, the way of living, mainly, the simplicity and contentment and great devotion to one's spiritual development.

There is no doubt he, as a Christian monk, knew quite deeply about Buddhism. He himself, you see, practiced some of the ideas of Buddhism, mainly to deal with meditation. Compassion, love, tolerance—these are the same for Christian and Buddhist. In Buddhism there are many systematic methods, how to develop step by step, mentioned in Buddhist scripture, so it's useful for the Christian to adopt some Buddhist ideas. And similarly for Buddhists to learn from Christian tradition. To help each other. It will help to enrich both traditions.

In our talks Merton said something we would both agree on: that spiritual beliefs are one of the major contributions for world peace. But I cannot say, and he did not say, that religion alone can achieve peace. There are many, many things, and no doubt religion is one of the key factors. But it is really through mental peace that there is a greater possibility to achieve real, lasting world peace. He could see, I could see, that if there are hateful feelings or extreme competitive attitudes, a genuine world peace is rather difficult. Through mental peace, through genuine sense of brotherhood, sisterhood, through that way, there is greater possibility to achieve real world peace. Mental peace comes through meditation, and he was a great teacher of meditation in the West.

You see, true religion must be a sort of destroyer. Compassion and tolerance, these we can call destroyers of anger. Destroyers of hatred. You can't remain with hatred if you know compassion. Yes, we were very serious in our discussions, but our nature, laughing, joking, teasing quickly came through. He had on this thick belt, very thick. I had only a cord, and my robes would always slip. And today my belt is also quite thick, but maybe not just like his. It is, how you say, a Macy copy. Practical, comfortable. Yes, in many ways, he was a wise man!

As a result of our discussions, I got a certain feeling I was with a person who had a great desire to learn. So I thought it quite fit, appropriate, to call him a Catholic *Geshe*. This means "a scholar" or "learned one." Also I could say he was a holy man. I don't know the exact Western interpretation of this term *holy,* but from a Buddhist viewpoint a holy person is one who sincerely implements what he knows. That we call *holy.* And, despite his knowledge or his position, lives a very simple way of life and is honest, and respects other people. I found these qualities in Thomas Merton.

When he died, I felt that I had lost personally one of my best friends, and a man who was a contributor for harmony between different religions and for mental peace. So we lost one, it is very sad. I think if he remained a longer period, I think if he remained still today, he would be one of my comrades to do something for mental peace, and for better understanding between Christians and Buddhists. I could learn still more from him. After all, here was a Christian monk who practiced and adopted Buddhist technique into Christian practice. One of the first, I believe, and so powerful in his writings, telling about it. In the Buddhist monks' community here in India we are learning about Christian tradition. And I personally am very much eager to copy from Christian tradition. Social work, social affairs, the education field: marvelous work. You see, in Buddhist tradition, we are, I should say, a bit neglectful about that aspect. We should learn these Christian traditions. Thomas Merton started me thinking this way. He opened my eyes. And now when I give talks, I often refer to Thomas Merton. He made a great impression on me.

When I think or feel something Christian, immediately his picture, his vision, his face comes to me. To the present day. Very nice.

Thich Nhat Hanh

I have far more in common with Nhat Hanh than I have with many Americans; I do not hesitate to say it. It is vitally important that such bonds be admitted. They are the bonds of a new solidarity and a new brotherhood which is beginning to be evident on all the five continents.

—*The NonViolent Alternative*

Thich Nhat Hanh is a Buddhist monk who was instrumental in the nonviolent movement of the United Buddhist Church during the war in his homeland, Vietnam. He has written a history of Buddhism in Southeast Asia and is well known for his book, The Miracle of Mindfulness. *Nhat Hanh lives in France and travels throughout the world speaking and giving retreats.*

It is hard to describe his face in words, to write down "This is what Thomas Merton was like." I can see it but I cannot describe it, but I can say that there was a lot of human warmth—*chaleur humaine*—in him. And conversation with him was so easy. When we talked, I told him a few things, and he understood the things I didn't tell him. Very nice. He was open to everything. I remember that I told him something about my being a Buddhist novice in Vietnam. About my life. And that was very interesting to him. He wanted to know more and more. He did not talk so much about himself. He was constantly asking questions. And then he would listen.

He had a good understanding of Buddhism. One of the most difficult things concerning the understanding between the East and West is that the West tends to think in a dualistic way. But in the East, if Buddha exists, then Marash (the god of Desire and Death) should exist also. Merton could see that the two are two faces of the same reality. And therefore we must not create a battle between them; we should have peace and reconciliation without making any effort. I don't remember everything that we talked about to each other, but I was impressed by his capacity of dialogue. I think, right in that night, he wrote the statement that "Nhat Hanh is my brother." I must confess that I did not sleep well because of the running water in the monastery. And I was so tired when I came to Gethsemani I lost my voice. We had to cancel my speech to the monks, so Tom suggested that I have lunch with the abbot. He said I didn't have to talk much. And also, he told me that I should not mind very much what the abbot said because he read *Time* magazine.

In the days that followed, when he would write me, he would always begin with "Dear Nhat." My name is Nhat Hanh, it means "one action." So he called me "Dear Nhat," which means "Dear One." Very nice. He said he felt closer to me than to a number of his Christian brothers. So my home can be his. Did he like to die there, in my area of the world? I don't know, because "Where was his home?" I would ask. It could be everywhere. I had a student who wrote a poem when she learned of the death of Thomas Merton. The idea is that there is a dove on the summit of a mountain; there is a chrysanthemum that blooms in the garden; there is a lightning, and "my master is home." She called Thomas Merton her master.

Thomas Merton was there in the monastery but he cannot be confined to that place. When you are a man of peace, even if you hide yourself in a mountain, you are working for peace. Because being in peace and working for peace is the same thing. If you are not peaceful, then how can you work for peace? Those who are in demonstrations, marches, like that, they may be less for peace than someone who is just in his quarters on a mountain.

It is like the Vietnamese Boat People when they cross the ocean. If the boat is caught in the tempest, and if there is one person who remains calm, lucid, there's no panic, and then all the people on the boat will profit from that. Maybe this one person does not do much, but his being there, calm, lucid, will save everyone. I don't make any distinction between being and doing. Sometimes we do very much, but not for the sake of peace. Sometimes we do not do anything, but we are for peace. So instead of saying, "Don't just sit there, do something," we can say the opposite: "Don't just do something, sit there."

Thomas Merton—his life, his feelings, his teachings, and his work—are enough to prove his courage, his determination, his wisdom. He did more for peace than many who were out in the world.

Jean Jadot

Yet it is in this loneliness that the deepest activities begin. It is here that you discover act without motion, labor that is profound repose, vision in obscurity, and, beyond all desire, a fulfillment whose limits extend to infinity.

—*New Seeds of Contemplation*

Jean Jadot, seventy-four, was granted his doctor of philosophy degree at Université Catholique, Louvain, Belgium, in 1930 and was ordained to the priesthood in 1934. In 1968 he was consecrated as bishop and assigned as apostolic pro nuncio for Thailand, Laos, Malaysia, and Singapore. In this capacity, he was in attendance at the Bangkok meeting at which Thomas Merton spoke. He served as nuncio in the United States from 1973 to 1980. Archbishop Jadot from 1980 to 1984, was President of the Vatican Secretariat for Non-Christians in Rome.

When I saw Merton for the first time on Monday morning, December 9, 1968, I didn't have any special impression, but on Tuesday when I returned to the Red Cross Center for his talk around eleven, I came a little earlier so we could talk. And I was struck, as I spoke with him, by the reddish color of his face. He started his address around eleven, and he slowly became more and more red. It was not a deep red, but still not a normal color. I remember coming out of the lecture with Abbot Weakland and telling him two things: First, that I was a little surprised by the way Thomas Merton was speaking—I had expected him to be a much easier and more dynamic speaker. And second, I was a little worried about the color of his face. I said this to get a reaction from Weakland. And he told me—I still remember—"Well, you know, he's not well." That was at noon on Tuesday, and he died two hours later.

When I met him on that Monday, I apologized for not being in

Bangkok when he arrived, and I asked him what had impressed him most in his travels. "Oh, it was India," he said, very excitedly, and I still have it in mind, as very often in the United States and elsewhere I've spoken about it. "What struck me and what I think we have to learn from India, is the importance of the guru, the master, the spiritual master." And he said very explicitly, "This is something we have lost in our Catholic tradition, and we have to return to it." He was really very convinced, insisting that for him it was one of the great lessons he had learned from his contacts with the spiritual men of India. You could see that something profound had happened to him.

When, years later, I went to Gethsemani to see his hermitage and I thought about him, his many writings, his many friends, those who looked to him for guidance, I was sure that he himself had the charisma of a guru. And I think that the training he got as a Trappist—a most ancient way—helped him to develop this charism he had. He did not seek to be a guru—it is not such a popular word, because it is often misused—but he was a great master himself.

As you try to place Merton in history, he is certainly in the trend of the post–Vatican II Church, but we must say that he was a presursor of Vatican II by the way he was opening himself to the other religions. He started first with the very closed Trappist life; he wanted nothing to do with anything but his own faith, and then slowly he opened himself. He opened himself first to non-Catholics and then to non-Christians, and was very much aware of the input and also the influx of the Eastern religions and Eastern cults in the United States and even in Europe. All that helped him to see at the beginning that there was something valuable to be found among those people. My impression in speaking with him, and reflecting on what he told me, was that he was more convinced that we had something to find in those non-Christian religions on *ways* and *means* rather than on real religious *truths*. If I may make use of an expression: We had more to find from them about *how* to pray than *what* to pray.

His place was not as a great thinker or philosopher, but more as somebody who had intuitions, feelings, the ability to see in what direction to go during a very troubled era.

For me he is a kind of prophet. And I think in the future he will be more remembered in the history of spirituality as a man who—I wouldn't say opened *new* ways—he reopened old ways we had forgotten. He had the ability to talk in new terms about things or attitudes or values that were common one thousand or fifteen hundred years ago.

I would place under three headings the values Merton restored or found a new approach to: First, our relationship with nature. Merton helped us to rediscover the cosmic dimension of our personalities. We are not men and women living alone, but we are living in a certain setting, a natural setting. And I think that his days in the East helped him to very strongly reinforce this conviction of the necessity for cultivating more harmony between man and nature; congeniality, not external but internal harmony. The second was that interiority is a very important dimension of human life. Modern life takes too much out of ourselves, making us busy with so many things, and doesn't give us time enough to think, to contemplate, meditate. Thomas Merton helped us to rediscover not a new but an old dimension of human life, which is interiority. That it is not so important to have; what is important is to be. Merton was really working, in his own language, in his own way of speaking and writing, helping people more to be than to have. This is where he was a guru, through his *words* and his presence in the flesh or in printed words. And the third value he helped to develop would be our relationship with others. Social life, I would say. But in a very special way, giving more importance to human relations, person-to-person; not a collective life, but a communal life. Not groups in society, but a human community.

I suppose that in the end his real role was to awaken people to the closeness in which we are living, the solidarity uniting all of us. Not only material solidarity, but spiritual solidarity too. Really, this notion of fellowship, the unity of humankind. We are all the same children of the same father. Not such a new thought, I would say, but he, the prophet, the guru, let us see it once again —and clearly.

Rembert G. Weakland

I have needed the experience of this journey. Much as the hermitage has meant, I have been needing to get away from Gethsemani and it was long overdue.   —*The Asian Journal of Thomas Merton*

Rembert G. Weakland, fifty-seven, joined the Benedictine Order in 1945, was ordained as a priest in 1951 and from 1966 to 1977 was Abbot Primate of the worldwide Benedictine Confederation. In this capacity he was one of the major organizers of the 1968 Bangkok Conference of Eastern and Western Monks, to which Thomas Merton traveled to deliver an address. In 1977, Abbot Weakland was appointed Archbishop of Milwaukee, an office he still holds.

At heart Merton was a romantic, in the good sense of the term. And the monastic ideal of the Trappists at that time was a rather romanticized notion of what monasticism was all about. The idea of total seclusion, of total silence, the long, flowing garments, the apple trees and the orchards. . . . I'm sure all of that, for him, was a fulfillment of many of his religious and romantic dreams. Since then the Trappists, like all of us, have changed, but at that time they corresponded to the journey he was making. Gethsemani was regarded as one of the most severe and rigorous monasteries in the world, a sort of Mount Everest to be climbed. And Merton wanted to climb it.

I read Merton and heard a lot about him when I finished up at Juilliard and attended Columbia University from 1953 to 1956. At that time his friend and mentor, Dan Walsh, was still around, and many others who had remembered Merton from his earlier years. I would say that most of them were a bit surprised at his move to Gethsemani and were very skeptical that he would stay. "He'll give it a try. . . ," they'd say, not being too convinced that it would be the ultimate home for Merton. There was great admiration for him, though. Great admiration. Everyone recognized his unusual talents, his insight, and his way of perceiving where things were spiritually.

In monastic circles, as I discovered when I became a monk myself, Merton had a powerful influence. He was considered an authentic voice for Western monasticism and Western contemplation. And so, when he moved in the 1950s toward the spirituality of the East and Eastern monasticism, he had to be taken very seriously, because here was a man who could appreciate the connections that others couldn't see or even scorned. The 1960s were very rough days for those of us interested in the East, and we knew that the success of the Bangkok meeting would depend much on who was going to be there. The attempt to get Merton was in the vein of "Well, it won't happen anyway, but let's try for the best." When he said yes, everybody was elated; we knew then that we would have a good meeting.

In fact, though, the meeting did not get off to a good start. There was much skepticism. The Buddhists had come but were highly controlled by their government, and it was very touch and go. Also, the French-speaking didn't trust the English-speaking. To top off all those tensions, I would say that most people were a bit disappointed in Merton. He was not a great speaker and in some respects not an attractive personality. He was not the kind of charismatic leader one might expect. He was a bit dull and had a certain standoffishness about him that threw a lot of people off. Some of them may have thought, "Well, it's pride." But I don't think it was. I think it was a natural tendency on his part to be a bit cautious and not assume the role of this great guru who suddenly appeared on the scene and whom everybody bowed to. He was nervous that day, there's no doubt about it. Don't forget, he had not appeared previously before television cameras and was definitely nervous about talking with that kind of publicity.

And then the big moment arrived; Merton came to the lectern. There was utter silence. Here was the most famous monk in the world about to share with us his profound thoughts. He wore his monastic habit, and I am sure it was hot in that lecture room. His delivery was clear and good—not excessively emotional, more like a class lecture.

At the end of the talk you could see it and feel it: people were disappointed. They had expected something closer to the problem we were talking about, which was the relationship between Eastern and Western mysticism. Instead, Merton seemed to talk more about the relationship between monasticism and Marxism. What's interesting to me is that at that moment nobody thought his talk was very germane; but five years later, when we came together at Bangalore, that talk was very much cited—probably because the problem of the monks at that moment was how to survive under communist domination. Our monks in Vietnam, our monks in Korea, all these—even the monks in India—were very interested in talking then about the relationship between monasticism and Marxism.

I wonder when he started writing that talk he gave at Bangkok. I have a suspicion that he started it after he was on his Asian journey, after he had visited some areas of the Orient and probably had seen the real conflict over there. It was not a monastic conflict. It was an ideological conflict between Marxists and capitalists, and therefore, he focused in on what monasticism would be about in that kind of world. And, as we've moved along since then, Merton's intuition, usually unerring, was proved correct again.

I was doing an interview with Dutch television when Abbot Haas burst in and said that something had happened to Merton. I followed him to one of the bungalows on the property owned by the Red Cross. Each bungalow had two stories; each floor was divided into four rooms with a hallway and temporary wooden walls up to about six feet with curtains above. Apparently one of the monks wanted to get the key to the bungalow because he was going into the city and would be coming home late. Merton kept the keys because his room was closest to the door. When the monk knocked on the panel to ask for the key, he got no response, but was able to look in and saw that there was a body on the floor. He called to the others living in the same building; they broke in.

The floor was made of terrazzo. The door to his shower was open, and the light there was on. When I arrived, which was a few minutes after that, they had already pulled out the plug of the fan that had fallen on the body. Abbot Haas, who had gotten a small shock when he pulled out the plug, said the fan was on the body with flames coming out of the fan when he came in.

Merton had only shorts on; it looked as if he had just taken a shower. He was on his back, stretched out, and there was a slight gash in the back of his head where his head had hit the floor. He was not holding the fan. It was a floor fan, probably about three and a half to four feet high, and the fan was on him, across him. There was a box where the velocity could be changed, and that box was right in the lower abdominal area, right against the flesh. The area around the box was burned pretty badly and that burn extended downward on the whole of the right side of Merton's body. Abbot Haas had with him the holy oils, so I anointed the body and performed the Rite of Extreme Unction. The body was still somewhat warm; it seemed to me that death had taken place only shortly before. I have to admit that Merton's contorted hands and feet struck me as being a sign that he had suffered in his dying. But although his face was distended, his expression was peaceful.

The doctors estimated death had occurred about half an hour before the body was found. It seemed evident to me that, if he had grabbed the fan and had been electrocuted in that fashion, he still would have been holding it. Instead, the body was flat, the hands and feet contorted as if he had tried to adjust the fan's controls, received a shock, and inadvertently pulled the fan on top of him as he fell backward.

After the discovery of the body and the anointing came all the difficulties with the police. We called the Thai police and coroner. It took about an hour and a half before they got there, and they did all the examining possible. They pronounced the death accidental, probably of a heart attack—although no one was really convinced of that.

You can imagine how everybody wants souvenirs; but I would not permit anybody to take or touch anything of his. The body was washed and dressed, and then came the problem of what to do with the body. Because of the heat in Thailand, one has twelve hours to make that kind of decision.

We phoned Abbot Flavian Burns at Gethsemani, and he said they wanted the body shipped back. But they also wanted an autopsy. What to me was incredible at the time, as I think back about it, was that the only morgue I could find to preserve the body was an American military morgue. And the only way to ship the body back was on an American military plane. An irony for a man who was so much for peace! We had a problem over the autopsy because I couldn't legally authorize it, and we couldn't get anything in writing from Abbot Burns within that time period. So the military doctors felt it was best to proceed with the embalming and, if they wanted an autopsy when the body arrived in San Francisco, that was a possibility but probably not a good one.

The next morning we had a beautiful Mass. I celebrated the Mass, and all the abbots celebrated along with me. Archbishop Jadot, the apostolic delegate in Thailand at the time, attended the Mass. Probably that was also the moment when our meeting came together. I probably have never preached a better sermon in my life. . . . I'm sure one rises to the occasion because of the emotional impact of something of this sort. We vowed to continue our meeting. That was our decision, that we didn't want to lose that moment to bring together who and what we were.

Merton's death was what brought everybody together. When the meeting was reconvened after his death, it was a totally different meeting. And that's hard to explain. But if you've been at meetings, you can see how sometimes something outside the actual program will bring people together and make it jell. And that did. Perhaps Merton can be considered a sacrificial lamb.

The sermon I gave was a moment of talking about Merton's search for God. When a monk enters a monastery, what is asked of him is "Are you truly seeking God?" The question isn't "Have you found God?" The question is "Is he seeking God? Is his motivation highly involved in that search of who and what God is in relationship to us?" It's not philosophical—it's existential. And Merton, to me, was a great searcher. He was constantly unhappy, as all great searchers are. He was constantly ill at ease, he was constantly restless, as all searchers are—because that's part of the search. And in that sense he was the perfect monk. Contemplation isn't satisfaction—it's search.

I am content that these pages show me to be what I am—noisy, full of the racket of my imperfections and passions, and the wide open wounds left by my sins. Full of my own emptiness. Yet, ruined as my house is, You live there! —*The Sign of Jonas*

Bibliography: Books by and about Thomas Merton

The following list of books by and about Thomas Merton contains the major and most readily obtainable works. For those who require scholarly or out-of-print books, or a more complete list, two sources are given at the end. When a price is noted (all are for paperback editions unless otherwise stated), the book is still in print. A short description of each book is provided whenever the title is not self-explanatory. For the person new to Merton, an asterisk (*) marks the entries that could make up a basic reading list. The year listed is the most recent edition.

BOOKS BY THOMAS MERTON

The Ascent to Truth. New York: Harcourt Brace, 1981. $6.95.
　　Theological reflections on St. John of the Cross and Carmelite spirituality.
The Asian Journal of Thomas Merton. Edited by Naomi Burton Stone, Patrick Hart, and James Laughlin. New York: New Directions, 1973. $7.25.
　　Merton's trip to the East in 1968.
A Blaze of Recognition: Merton Day by Day. Edited by Thomas P. McDonnell. New York: Doubleday, 1983. $14.95 (hardcover).
　　Quotes from Merton books arranged for daily reading and meditation.
A Catch of Anti-Letters. By Thomas Merton and Robert Lax. Kansas City, MO: Sheed, Andrews & McMeel, 1978.
　　Correspondence between two lifelong friends.
The Climate of Monastic Prayer. Kalamazoo, Mich.: Cistercian Publications, 1973. $7.95.
The Collected Poems of Thomas Merton. New York: New Directions, 1980. $18.95.
Conjectures of a Guilty Bystander. New York: Doubleday, 1966. $5.95.
　　Random thoughts in the 1960s.
Contemplation in a World of Action. New York: Doubleday, 1973. $5.50.
　　Combining a life of prayer and action.
Contemplative Prayer. New York: Doubleday, 1971. $2.95.
　　Practical guide.

Disputed Questions. New York: Farrar, Straus & Giroux, 1960, $12.50.
    Prayer and action in modern society.
Faith & Violence: Christian Teaching & Christian Practice. Notre Dame,
    Ind.: University of Notre Dame Press, 1968. $4.95.
Geography of Lograire. New York: New Directions, 1969. $4.95.
    Merton's epic poem.
Introductions East & West: The Foreign Prefaces of Thomas Merton. Edited by
    Robert E. Daggy. Greensboro, N.C.: Unicorn Press, 1981.
    $7.50.
The Last of the Fathers: Saint Bernard of Clairvaux & the Encyclical Letter,
    Doctor Mellifluus. New York: Harcourt Brace, 1981. $4.95.
Life & Holiness. New York: Doubleday, 1963.
    Spiritual meditations.
The Literary Essays of Thomas Merton. Edited by Patrick Hart. New York:
    New Directions, 1981. $39.95.
The Living Bread. New York: Farrar, Straus & Giroux, 1956. $5.95.
Love & Living. Edited by Naomi Burton Stone and Patrick Hart. New
    York: Farrar, Straus & Giroux, 1979. $10.00.
*_The Monastic Journey._ Edited by Patrick Hart. New York: Doubleday,
    1978. $3.95.
    Collection of articles and essays on monastic life.
My Argument with the Gestapo: A Macaronic Journal. New York: New Di-
    rections, 1975. $6.95.
    Early, partially autobiographic work of fiction.
The New Man. New York: Bantam Books, 1981. $1.95.
    Probing one's spiritual self.
*_New Seeds of Contemplation._ Revised Edition. New York: New Direc-
    tions, 1972. $4.95.
    Merton's spiritual classic; short meditations.
No Man Is an Island. New York: Harcourt Brace, 1978. $4.95.
    Looking at various aspects of the spiritual life.
The Nonviolent Alternative. New York: Farrar, Straus & Giroux, 1980.
    $7.95.
    Writings on peace and nonviolence.
Original Child Bomb. Greensboro, N.C.: Unicorn Press, 1983. $4.95.
    Prose poem on the Atomic bomb; illustrated with Merton's abstract art.
Raids on the Unspeakable. New York: New Directions, 1970. $4.95.
    Prose and poems concerning the contemporary scene.
Seasons of Celebration. New York: Farrar, Straus & Grioux, 1978. $6.95.
    Insights and meditations on the liturgical year.
The Secular Journal. New York: Farrar, Straus & Giroux, 1959. $3.95.
    Diarylike collection written just before Merton entered the Trappists.
Seeds of Destruction. New York: Farrar, Straus & Giroux, 1964. $6.95.
    Merton on race and discrimination.

Selected Poems. New York: New Directions, 1967. $4.95.
*The Seven Storey Mountain. New York: Harcourt Brace, 1978. $6.95.
    Merton's autobiographical classic.
*The Sign of Jonas. New York: Harcourt Brace, 1979. $4.95.
    Journal of daily life at Gethsemani, 1946–1952.
The Silent Life. New York: Farrar, Straus & Giroux, 1975. $4.95.
    Of monks and monasticism.
Thomas Merton on St. Bernard. Kalamazoo, MI: Cistercian Publications, 1980. $4.95.
    Introduction by Jean Leclercq.
Thoughts in Solitude. New York: Farrar, Straus & Giroux, 1976. $3.95.
The Waters of Siloe. New York: Harcourt Brace, 1979. $4.95.
    A history of the monastic order of Cistercians.
The Way of Chuang Tzu. New York: New Directions, 1969. $3.95.
    On the Chinese master; with Merton's calligraphies.
What is Contemplation? Springfield, IL: Templegate, 1981. $4.95.
*Wisdom of the Desert. New York: New Directions, 1970. $3.95.
    Translations of some sayings of the early Desert Fathers, who were precursors of monasticism.
Woods, Shore, Desert: A Notebook, May 1968. Albuquerque: University of New Mexico Press, 1983. $6.95.
    Merton in the American West shortly before his death.
Zen & the Birds of Appetite. New York: New Directions, 1968. $4.95.
    The "study" of Zen; and D. T. Suzuki.

BOOKS ABOUT THOMAS MERTON

Raymond Bailey. *Thomas Merton on Mysticism.* New York: Doubleday, 1976. $1.95.
James T. Baker. *Thomas Merton:* Social Critic. Lexington: University Press of Kentucky, 1971. $17.00 (hardcover).
Marquita Elaine Breit. Thomas Merton: A Bibliography. Metuchen, N.J.: Scarecrow Press, 1974.
Richard A. Cashen. *Solitude in the Thought of Thomas Merton.* Kalamazoo, Mich.: Cistercian Publications, 1981. $5.50.
David R. Collins. *Thomas Merton: Monk with a Mission.* Cincinnati, Ohio: St. Anthony Messenger Press, 1981.
    Young person's guide to Merton.
**James H. Forest. *Thomas Merton: A Pictorial Biography.* Ramsey, N.J.: Paulist Press, 1980. $5.95.
**Monica Furlong. *Merton: A Biography.* New York: Bantam Books, 1981. $3.95.

John Howard Griffin. *The Hermitage Journals: A Diary Kept While Working · on the Biography of Thomas Merton.* New York: Doubleday, 1983. *Merton's first biographer.*

John H. Griffin. *A Hidden Wholeness: The Visual World of Thomas Merton.* Boston: Houghton Mifflin, 1979. $7.95.

*Patrick Hart. *The Message of Thomas Merton.* Kalamazoo, MI: Cistercian Publications, 1981. $5.50.

*Patrick Hart. *Thomas Merton, Monk: A Monastic Tribute.* Cistercian Publications, 1983. $7.95. *The many facets of Thomas Merton.*

John J. Higgins. *Thomas Merton on Prayer.* New York: Doubleday, 1975. $3.95.

Ross Labrie. *The Art of Thomas Merton.* Fort Worth: Texas Christian University Press, 1979. $9.95.

Therese Lentfoehr. *Words & Silence: On the Poetry of Thomas Merton.* New York: New Directions, 1979. $4.95.

*Michael Mott. *The Seven Mountains of Thomas Merton.* Boston: Houghton Mifflin, 1984. $24.95. *Authorized Merton biography.*

Henri J. Nouwen. *Thomas Merton: Contemplative Critic.* New York: Harper & Row, 1981. $5.75.

Anthony T. Padovano. *Contemplation & Compassion: Thomas Merton's Vision.* Peter Pauper Press, 1984. $3.95. *Short meditations on Merton's spirituality.*

Anthony T. Padovano. *The Human Journey: Thomas Merton, Symbol of the Century.* New York: Doubleday, 1982. $13.95 (hardcover). *A Study of Merton as Monk and Writer.*

*Edward E. Rice. *The Man in the Sycamore Tree: The Good Times and Hard Life of Thomas Merton.* New York: Doubleday, 1970. *A good friend looks at Merton.*

*William H. Shannon. *Thomas Merton's Dark Path: The Inner Experience of a Contemplative.* New York: Farrar, Straus & Giroux, 1981. $5.95.

Cornelia Sussman and Irving Sussman. *Thomas Merton.* New York: Doubleday, 1980. $3.95. *Juvenile biography.*

*Paul Wilkes. *Merton: By Those Who Knew Him Best.* New York: Harper & Row, 1984. $12.95 (hardcover). *Reflections of his closest friends; taken from interviews for Merton, a film biography of Thomas Merton.*

George Woodcock. *Thomas Merton—Monk & Poet: A Critical Study.* New York: Farrar, Straus & Giroux, 1978. $3.95.

For Merton books, both in- and out-of-print, and a catalogue:

Bardstown Art Gallary
310 Xavier Drive
P.O. Box 417
Bardstown, KY 40004
(502) 348-6488

For a more complete listing of books by and about Thomas Merton and information on Merton research:

Thomas Merton Studies Center
Bellarmine College
Louisville, KY 40205
(502) 452-8187

MERTON: A Film Biography of Thomas Merton, a one hour documentary, aired throughout the public television network in 1984 and is available in film and video tape through:

First Run Features   and Mass Media Ministries
153 Waverly Place   2116 No. Charles Street
New York, NY 10014   Baltimore, MD 21218
(212) 243-0600   (301) 727-3270